BE A
COSMIC CH
IN THE ERA O

QUANTO SHIVO

**Published and Distributed by
Quanto Publishing**

Address: Quanto Publishing
D-1204, Mohar Pratima, Rao Colony, Talegaon, Pune 410506

E-mail: dwaparsadhana@gmail.com
Website: www.beacosmicchannel.com

CONTENTS

ACKNOWLEDGMENTS

My deepest gratitude to the Quanto vibrational field for its guidance and synchronicities.

To the Quanto family for continuous love, trust, support, enthusiasm and participation in the project.

To Quanto Mansi, co-founder of Quanto Life, for being the inspiration and the heartthrob of Quantos which has knit this family together and for being my writing companion.

To Vyjayanti Tejuja, project head for her commitment, excitement and skillful coordination.

To Jayalakshmi Chittoor for bringing in her vast expertise and experience and guiding us through various crucial junctures.

To the workshop participants for their deep trust. They opened their hearts out during those 21 days of intense dialogue and self-enquiry. Their vulnerability and courage took this workshop to a level that we never imagined was possible at the time when we started the workshop. They even allowed us to share some of their private conversations for the benefit of all. It is through their sincere sharing and seeking that this book took life and came into being. Most of these participants will be introduced in some detail in the forthcoming book.

To the transcription team – Latha Kumar, Nitika Sethi, Nishtha Maru, Kawal Sethi, Daisy Talreja, Jyotsna Sarwaikar, Pallavi Arondekar, Rashi Aggarwal, Vaibhav Aggarwal, Jyoti Sharma, Aruna Puri, Vyjayanti Tejuja for their word-to-word transcription of each day of the workshop.

To the editing team, Quanto Mansi, Jayalakshmi Chittoor, Uttara Srinivas and Jaya Yadav, for their commitment towards bringing out an excellent book and yet adopting new ideas into a task that is considered traditional.

To Uttara Srinivas, Atin Tripathi for their contribution in terms of ideas and technical skill towards cover page design concepts.

To Suchismita Banerjee for her enthusiasm to develop strategy and lead the social media team.

To Kshitij Johri, Ajay Sarwaikar, Rupali Kari, Amit Raheja for being part of the ideation and coordination.

To our publishing consultant Shiv Ganesh Prajapati for sharing his experience, guidance and bringing the book into physical form.

To True Sign Publishing House for their end-to-end support in the publishing journey.

Cover page image credit: ESA/NASA/JPL-Caltech, Image from Herschel Space Telescope (ESA)

To the ambassadors who valued the book and shared and spread it to a larger group in their respective areas of influence.

You are all my co-creators on this journey.

WHY IS THIS BOOK SO IMPORTANT?

Post 1997 Chaotic World

This book is extremely vital and important because it explains a simple *sutra* for survival of humanity through the extremely chaotic and challenging times post 1997. The seeding for such eventful times happened in 1981 and it gained full momentum by 1997. This time is likely to continue for another 500-1000 years. In such times of crises, the old way of resolving conflicts through thinking/contemplation and future projection has been rendered largely ineffective. This book proposes an alternate resolution mechanism through "Grounding in Space" and "Being A Cosmic Channel" for every crisis as well as for new creations. It shows the way to download your own personal guidance for various individual and collective issues as you live through these intense times on a continual basis.

2012 Mayan Prophecy was About this Plasmic Transit

Since 1997, our solar system has entered the infinity like galactic equator as shown in the cover page picture (Image credit: ESA/NASA/JPL- Caltech. Image from Herschel Space telescope).

Such a transit happens almost once every 12000 years for a duration of 500-1000 years, and has huge ramifications for planet earth and its inhabitants, especially us humans. Understanding this phenomenon and its repercussions warrants one whole book in itself, but let me explain the essence of this in brief. This transit has opened up our solar system and earth to the outer influences of infinite objects existing in the whole of the galaxy. The evolution of planet earth and human race to where it is currently has been largely driven by many of such past transits. Also as earth began to get bombarded with huge plasmic energy, electrical conductivity of the environment multiplied manifold. It has integrated the whole of humanity into one collective whole, and such a longing for oneness is manifested as the Internet. This has opened huge opportunities for us humans to grow in spiritual, psychic and occult capabilities and understand ourselves and life much deeper. Humongous amount of new knowledge has descended to the extent that just in 25 years we have created more knowledge than all the accumulated knowledge of the past 5000 years.

Yet this plasmic inflow has also posed the greatest challenge humanity has ever faced. Geological records suggest that electromagnetic fields of earth could rise to such an extent that are impossible for us humans to bear. The Story of *Matsya Avatar* in which *Vishnu* reincarnates as a fish to save the seed of humanity, and many other such stories from across the world, corroborated by geological evidence, points to the catastrophic ramifications of this phenomenon. Undirected intense plasmic flow, unabsorbed by earth's electromagnetic field, is giving rise to natural disasters that are becoming ever more intense. The whole of humanity now faces an existential crisis. Intense plasma flowing through the earth is now entering human aura; igniting the destructive volcano-like forces hidden in individual and collective subconscious and giving rise to instantaneously triggered social, national and religious mega conflicts.

Synchronistically, the advanced Mayan culture had also made a prophecy that foretold of a time of recalibration of humanity - a grand new beginning and great changes that would happen in 2012. The modern astronomical calculations revised that date to 1997 which ties the Mayan prophecy to the plasmic transit.

Ascending Yuga: From Survival to Creation

In 1895 Sri Yukteswar, the Guru of Paramhansa Yogananda, in his book "The Holy Sciences" declared that we had already entered the *Ascending Dwapar Yuga* in the early 18th century. This is in complete contradiction to the existing popular belief that we are in *Kali Yuga*. And yet, Sri Yukteswar's declaration seemed rational to me. So I extensively researched astronomical causes of the *Yuga cycle* and scientific evidence of how it impacts life and have furthered this work. This is again a subject of one full book that I intend to write about in the near future.

The whole of recorded human history of the past 10000 years belongs to the descending/low consciousness phase of the *Yuga cycle*. This phase had two major ramifications in terms of how it shaped human thinking: first, the past is always better than future; second, survival is the prime concern of humanity, and hence every social concept, moral belief and spiritual method was geared towards ensuring survival. Now we are in the ascending consciousness phase of the *Yuga cycle* where the future is better than the past and creation is the primary human motivation. Such a future demands a whole new paradigm for social, political, economic and spiritual understanding.

Lighthouse in the Current Era of Chaos

The two astronomical factors - the plasmic transit and the *Ascending Dwapar Yuga* makes current consciousness radically different from all prior times. As the reality of the world has evolved, even our understanding of spiritual journey has to take a leap. This book takes the ancient concept of *Aham Brahmasmi* to a whole new level of "Be the Cosmic Channel". The current consciousness is more alive, vibrant and evolved. The plasmic transit makes this current time intense and chaotic. The pace of life is very hectic and the sense of predictability of the future is lost. Hence, in the present times, the usual tools of thinking, strategising, and making choices have been rendered ineffective. This requires a whole new understanding for empowered living - "Grounding in Space". Triggering of the subconscious is always extremely intense and difficult to deal with. However, it can cleanse a huge storehouse of *karma*, dissolving the only block to experiencing *Aham Brahmasmi*. This is a true blessing.

Hindu Dharma, the only evolution centric religion in the world, provides us with the understanding that challenges are the fuel for evolutionary mechanisms (Plasma poses the greatest challenge humanity has ever encountered.). If humanity can cross this plasmic challenge, it would have taken a quantum leap towards collectively evolving into a race of super humans, as envisaged in ancient *Hindu* scriptures. However, our failure would mean that human civilisation, once again, would be swallowed by the fury of nature in the not too distant future.

Spiritual Insights of Quantum Science and String Theory

Quantum science suggests that manifestation of reality depends on the consciousness of the observer. More conscious the observation, the higher the manifestation. String theory mentions vibrations as the cause of every manifestation in the world. Integration of both would imply that more conscious observation of individual and collective vibrational reality, would empower us to play a greater role towards a better world.

This vibrational reality has often been referred to as the causal body *(Karan sharir)* in Hindu philosophy - the fourth layer of the seven layered reality of the cosmos. For the past few thousand years, the causal body remained a theoretical concept as the real experience of the causal body was almost impossible. So for all masters from the past, the spiritual techniques were mostly based on breathing which is a subtle body phenomenon that includes *chakras* (the second body). Typically, masters/spiritual practices avoided entering the emotional body - the third body. Probably that is why women - more emotional than men- were largely prohibited from spiritual practices. Buddha introduced *Vipassana* which is a third body practice but he had to withdraw it since it caused immense pain and suffering for seekers at that stage of *Kaliyuga* consciousness. Now in the current times of high consciousness, the vibrational reality is much more accessible and hence the spiritual tool for dissolving the emotions stored in the subconscious can be better applied. Hence observation of vibrational reality is viable in current times.

Aham Brahmasmi is the Peak Practical Wisdom for Current Times

Upanishads have been held in highest regard by various masters through the ages. Quantum sciences explain ancient *Upanishadic* wisdom in the modern context of *ascending Yuga*. The following quotes by great quantum scientists can help us to understand the value of *Upanishadic* wisdom in current times:

"Most of my ideas and theories are heavily influenced by *Vedanta (Upanishads)*" - Erwin Schrodinger.

"After the conversations about Indian philosophy, some of the ideas of Quantum physics that seemed so crazy suddenly made more sense" - Werner Heisenberg.

"I go into the *Upnishads* to ask questions" - Neils Bohr

Upanishads provide deep inquiry and insights into the deepest of the questions/subjects we face in life. **Aham Brahmasmi** *(I am God)* is the peak of *Upanishadic* wisdom which suggests the highest state of being humans can accomplish. Till now this wisdom had been considered highly esoteric which was meant only for a chosen few. However, the current times of chaos necessitates that this wisdom is applied on a regular basis by the masses.

Hence this book.

THE JOURNEY OF THE BOOK

Seeding of this Book

This book was seeded when I had my own **Aham Brahmasmi** experience in 2009. Until then, I had resisted giving teachings to anyone even though many people insisted. I would refuse saying, do I really know anything that I can teach you? A few days after my **Aham Brahmasmi** experience, I received a cosmic download that revealed one of my ancient past lives. In that life, I was a world famous teacher whose life and teachings continue to have a massive impact even in the modern world we live in. That is when I realised my own responsibility to the world and let go of my resistance.

Conscious Pilgrimage, Mystical Experiences

The second important turning point came with my visit to Vyas caves near Badrinath in uttarakhand india in 2012 where vibrational fragments of a significant past life of mine got re-integrated with my then vibrational state. That allowed me to access the talents, networks as well as the challenges of that life. I experienced a psychic download of various Hindu metaphysical concepts like *Yuga cycles*, nature of gods and goddesses as mentioned in the *Puranas* and the evolutionary nature of life.

Meeting of Paradoxes - Quantum Science and Metaphysics

Just a few weeks later, I was mystically guided towards Sri Yukteswar's declaration about the dawn of *Ascending Yuga* contrary to the all pervasive popular belief in India that we are in *Kaliyuga* and far worse times are yet to come. I was shocked, stunned and awed. Strangely, this information came to me through the website of a Quantum scientist, Dr Amit Goswami. The fact, that information of the *Yuga cycle* was published by a Quantum scientist gave it more credibility. This juxtaposition of Quantum science and *Yuga cycle* intrigued me. It propelled me towards further research into its astronomical origin, electromagnetic fields, human history and how it would shape the future of human evolution.

The Origin Story of Quanto

Around 2013, I was obsessed with Quantum sciences so much that I even explained astrology through Quantum sciences. Mansi often teased me by calling me by the name "Quanto". This quickly caught on with the other students too. Even though it began as a joke, I loved the nickname so much that I added it to my spiritual name Shivo. The sound of Quanto appeared vibrant and enticing - so much in harmony with the current consciousness that it became the name of the ensuing spiritual path and the vibrational field.

Oneness

I was fascinated that the spiritual mystical experiences happening to me could be very well explained by Quantum sciences. As I researched the astronomical origin of *Yuga cycles*, it became clear that the consciousness of the ascending phase is starkly different from the consciousness of the descending phase. This also revealed radical insights on how human society is going to evolve in future.

As this new reality got included in my understanding, even the current social trends which are condemned such as breaking of families, rising divorce rates, pre and extra marital sex started to appear as a phenomenon that is cleansing of the past and allowing more evolved social constructs.

As I realised the evolutionary mechanism of life, a deep acceptance of the world happened. The world and the divine were merging into one. In that oneness, there was a respect for traditional spiritual practices that had worked in the past but also the realisation that they are no more effective in current times. A new evolution oriented spiritual path was descending on me. The Epicurean riddle that had always haunted the spiritually inclined, myself included, now got resolved (this is discussed in detail later in the book).

Burning Question: Why Evil often Emerges Victorious over Good?

This also resolved my two-decade old burning question - why does evil often emerge victorious over good? The answer I received appeared so potent. Could this be the key for a wonderful future where power and resources, mostly accumulated in the hands of the evil, shift back into the hands of the good? This could be the key to bring heaven on earth. And I started to teach this. I had been having numerous mystical experiences with *rishised, avatars, sages, gurus* but none of this could prepare me for what came next. It was way beyond my wildest nightmares. I found myself in the psychic spheres where dark forces engulfed me. They wanted me to stop empowering the good. This was an extremely hellish experience which lasted continuously for five years. For a long time, every night I pleaded to *Lord Shiva* to give me death hoping that death would free me from this ordeal. There was even a period of 3-4 months, where I had almost no sleep, even a 15 minute nap during the whole of 24 hours would appear like a divine blessing. Then an even more sinister fear arose - what if these forces captured me after death? I deeply trusted that the divine would liberate me from this even if I get trapped in such a world for thousands of years. I even warned Mansi that they could draw my soul out of my body and insert another sinister soul and if that happens, how to identify and what to do after that? This may make me sound like a complete lunatic, and yet it opened a door in a new dimension. Gods and goddesses in vibrational forms started to descend to free me even though in my earlier spiritual practices I had hardly bothered about them. A mega war ensued in the psychic dimension and went on for years. However, this turned out to be a great blessing as it provided the kind of intensity that was necessary for the creation of what came to be later known as the Quanto Vibrational Field (QVF). The intensity needed to create a vibrational field is akin to high temperatures needed for nuclear fusion on the sun. And Quanto Life was born.

From Making of the Workshop to the Making of the Book

In the course of 6 years, we have created and regularly conducted many workshops which were hugely transformational. Participants rapidly progressed on their spiritual journey, experienced miracles and discovered whole new dimensions of their existence. The soulful Quanto family got created that loved, celebrated and trusted each other.

Some of the committed Quanto *sadhaks* had been ready for a leap and in this context, the ***"Aham Brahmasmi - Be a Cosmic Channel"*** workshop was born. Almost every participant had a glimpse of the ultimate reality. With this grand leap, their lives were transformed forever. This workshop, like every other workshop created in the Quanto field, continues to exist in the Quanto Vibrational Field and is available to those who can connect with it.

The Mission of the Book

It is the love and the blessing of the divine that has been preparing me through conscious pilgrimages, hellish as well as heavenly interactions in the psychic world, remembrances of past lives, various synchronicities in metaphysical and intellectual spheres, astronomical and astrological understanding, and the coming together of evolved, talented and highly committed souls that has synthesised into this project. There was a huge realisation among participants that the Grounding in Space - the most vital *sutra* imbibed in the workshop could be the key for the future of human evolution through the most challenging and yet potent times ahead. And for that the *sutra* of Grounding in Space must reach the masses.

And hence the Book.

ABOUT THE BOOK
HOWTO USE THE BOOK

The Interactive Format: Many Masters, One Method

All over the world, through the ages, masters have transmitted their wisdom through interaction with their disciples. Ancient texts such as *Upanishads* and Dhammapada (Buddha's discourses) as well as contemporary ones such as "I am That" by Nisaraga Dutt Maharaj, "Who am I" by Ramana Maharshi, "the Power of Now' by Eckart Tolle employ the same format. Why is it so?

Interaction is the most *sahaj* (effortless) way for transmission

The experience of the ultimate reality, Aham Brahmasmi, is so vast, so infinite, that it is futile to even attempt to put words to it. So when masters have this experience, they go into silence. If they ever attempted to describe it, it would become another intellectual concept turned into an ego tool in the hands of their followers that would eventually become a new block for spiritual seekers.

In the presence of a realised master, they sensed the bliss and that created a desire in them to experience it. This deepened their spiritual journey. They started to look at their lives in a whole new context and with that arose many questions which they posed to their master. The questions they asked were based on their interpretation of the life they lived and through those questions - the master was able to see where they were, what their blocks were and responded to them in a way that dissolved their blocks.

Answer the Questioner not the Question

Osho was often asked why he gave contradictory answers to the same question. Osho famously replied that he addressed the questioner and not the question. This was Osho's way to break the intellectual concept that had become their block. For example, to a person who was guilty about money, he would say money is divine, it is a gift, a blessing. To a person who was greedy, he would say money is a burden - what is it going to give you, why are you so possessive about it?

Similarly, Buddha responded in contradiction when he was asked about the existence of God. To an atheist, he would say there is God and to a believer, he would say there is no God. Why? Because, both were talking from their beliefs, intellectual concepts and not from their real experience and Buddha wanted to break it so that they can jump into a real experience.

So the masters responded based on where the questioner was on the journey and what his next step could be. So in essence, they did not explain their own concept rather they tried to dissolve the concepts their disciples held.

Decoding Gita: The Song of God

The *Gita* is the crescendo of all such master disciple interactions. In the words of the great quantum scientist Erwin Schrodinger "the *Bhagavad Gita* is the most beautiful philosophical song existing in any known tongue".

Typically, the disciple asks the master a question based on a situation he has already lived in the past. The master's answer will be interpreted and applied by the disciple on a life situation in future. The question came from the past but the answer will be applied in the future. In contrast, the Gita happens in the current moment - in the here and now. With the greatest hero of the age, *Arjuna* facing his existential crisis and the greatest master *Krishna* at his side, at peak intensity - the brink of the greatest war of the age that includes all the kings and kingdoms of that ecosystem, a culmination of vengeance across more than three generations, and a fight unto decimation of one side.

At its core, *The Gita* is a dialogue between *Krishna* and *Arjuna*. They begin their relationship as almost equals with *Krishna* as a friend, philosopher and guide. *Krishna* comes again to his rescue as many doubts laced with guilt surface in Arjun's mind. Even though *Krishna* is answering *Arjuna's* questions with a lot of patience, *Arjuna* is not really listening but rather continuously justifies his stand. A lot of wisdom is flowing in this conversation but *Arjuna* is not satiated. As this continues, *Krishna* realises that this Q & A can be endless and inconclusive. That's when *Krishna* shows His *Vishwarupa* (cosmic form) and in that awe, the surrender happens to *Arjuna*. At that moment - a new relationship happens - not just of a master and disciple but of a God and His devotee.

Krishna The Avatar (Cosmic Channel)

If *Arjuna*, the superhero of the age, would not fight, there was no chance that this war would happen. *Arjuna* was ready to give up; *Krishna* persuaded him to follow his dharma and fight. So the entire burden of karma - of the countless innocent people who would perish in this war would be on *Krishna*. So what made *Krishna* take this on?

The answer is simple. *Krishna* had received the cosmic message that the war was God's wish. *Krishna* tried everything he could to stop the war. As a last ditch effort, he asked *Duryodhana* that even if he could give 5 villages to *Pandavas*, *Krishna* would convince them. But *Duryodhana* flatly refused and declared that he would not even give land equivalent to the tip of a needle to *Pandavas*. Till this point, *Krishna* had understood the huge price of war and had been trying to stop, but at this point, He stopped trying. He becomes clear that war is the cosmic wish. And this is the moment of cosmic channeling.

To get a glimpse of the ultimate reality, *Aham Brahmasmi,* and to channel it, is what makes one a cosmic channel. To do so, even once in a lifetime is a fulfillment of many lifetimes of evolution. *Krishna* lives as a cosmic channel in every moment. That is why He is an *Avatar*. That is why He is our inspiration.

Universal Timeless Appeal of *Gita*

The beauty of cosmic channeling is that it is not just divine wish *(seventh chakra)* - it is not just psychic *(sixth chakra)* - it's not just divine knowledge *(fifth chakra)*- it's not just unconditional love *(fourth chakra)*- it is also about resolving the power struggle *(third chakra)*, the transactional issues *(second chakra)* and the fight for survival *(first chakra)*. So, the *Gita* can be received through all the seven *chakras* - so you receive a message at whatever level of evolution you are at. It has a divinity that this war is the wish of God. The overwhelming psychic revelation through *Vishwaswarupa*, the plethora of divine knowledge, the surrender of a devotee *Arjuna* which descends in the world ensuring that the good win against the evil, to resolve the family, property and social issues, ensuring the survival of humanity through the tough times of *Kaliyuga* that were to come.

The Leela of Life - the Unfolding of Spiritual Drama

1. There is also a rare category of books such as *Kathamrit* - "the darshan diaries" by M.K. Gupta - where people are not asking questions, rather they are sharing the reality of their lives. And in the presence of the mesmerising, charismatic *Ramakrishna Paramahamsa*, a spiritual drama unfolds and the person gets transformed.

2. "Republic" - A book by Plato is considered one of the most influential works of philosophy. This book is also in the form of dialogue and a drama wherein various real life characters are discussing different

concepts and life situations. Socrates tests their beliefs, concepts and justifications related with many diverse subjects such as - love, aging, politics, justice, death on pure logic. Through logic, he exposes the lacunas in understanding. Before Socrates, logic had largely degenerated into referencing from ancient scriptures. This book became the seed of rational thinking that led to the scientific revolution and modern society. Socrates coined the word Philosophy that meant love for truth; the Socratic method is about exploring truth through pure logic.

This Book is Similar yet Different

This book has some similarities with all the above mentioned formats. While most spiritual books cover two genres, this book integrates a triad of genres - self evolution (self-development), spiritual and metaphysical (new radical concepts). Participants are sharing from the past and yet many new events are unfolding as the workshop progresses. It is also set in a modern world - increasingly chaotic and intense - the context of which is hugely different from all the above mentioned books with its insights on identity paradoxes and subconscious dissolution. There are interactions on intellectual queries but it is also interspersed with channeled metaphysical concepts/ new knowledge.

A Portal into the Glimpse of the Ultimate Reality *Aham Brahmasmi*

This book imitates life. In our lives, from hour to hour, day to day, we move from one thing to another. However, there is one common thread that - life is happening. This book shows how we can get grounded in our daily life. And through living your daily life, you can begin to have glimpses of the ultimate reality - *Aham Brahmasmi.*

This book discusses many subjects and events. These subjects can be mundane or intense - ordinary or extraordinary. And through all or any one of these subjects, you can begin to have glimpses of the ultimate reality - *Aham Brahmaasmi.*

This book holds the real life stories that have happened, are happening and will happen to all the participants and the readers. They include heart to heart sharing, eruption of subconscious and its dissolution, life after life patterns and triggers, and through all or any of these emotions and experiences, you can get a glimpse of *Aham Brahmasmi*.

How to Read this Book

Even though content has been edited and footnotes have been added for clarity, we have made every possible attempt to keep the original voice of the participants that reflects their emotions. To keep this emotional tone alive, we have largely kept the original words and sentence formation. We have preferred authenticity of voices over grammatical perfections. So, tune into the essence and go easy on the grammar. Each participant represents thousands/ millions of people across the world. It is very likely that you will relate with one or more participants. We have also adopted the "three dots" format "..." as a reminder for you to pause and ponder. It is recommended to invoke the Quanto Vibrational Field by saying the words Quanto Quanto Quanto, before starting to read the book, as well as at any point where you experience a deep resonance or intensity.

Apart from being a portal, this book is also a divination tool like the magical book "The Autobiography of a Yogi". You can receive guidance on a day-to-day basis or any issue.

> *"Close your eyes*
>
> *Ask your question,*
>
> *Invoke the Quanto Vibrational Field*
>
> *Quanto Quanto Quanto*
>
> *Open any page*
>
> *That is your guidance*
>
> *From the cosmos"*

Relevance for All

All deva souls will feel empowered and find deeper spiritual connection.

Students/professionals/teachers will discover their way to receive career guidance on an ongoing basis.

Entrepreneurs will find a way to make empowered choices in tune with the future which is largely unpredictable.

Scientists will discover pointers to new revelations that are more in harmony with the current unfolding reality of life.

All creative people such as artists, writers, etc. will channel new unprecedented forms of creative expression and inspiration.

Parents will channel guidance on how to nurture the unique potential of their children and prepare them for success in a world they as parents will never know.

Healers will download a burst of healing vibrations.

Occult/metaphysical practitioners/philosophers will receive insights on how life works and what will be relevant for the future.

Media professionals will receive the collective understanding of the segments they are dealing with.

Celebrities/influencers will connect with the aspirations of their audiences.

These are just a few examples but each and every person reading this book will be empowered to deal with a future that is largely uncertain, discover their heroic potential and impact the world in unprecedented ways.

SYNOPSIS: GOD IS NOT JUST ESOTERIC, BUT ALSO PRACTICAL

(largely based on the interaction that took place on 2nd April 2023 during the online event World Transformation Day)

- Upanishadic understanding of God is harmonious with the key Quantum concept.

- The divine and ego in terms of vibrational realities.are in contrast with each other.

- It is critical to know that *Kaliyuga* has ended and we are already in ascending *Dwapar Yuga*.

- Chaos is originating from the transit of earth through the infinity like galactic disc, the zone of plasma.

- Grounding in Space is the simple and natural way to make empowered choices even in complicated situations.

- Synchronicities flow, when you surrender your dreams and follow the dreams God has for you.

- Listening to Your Heart is a spiritual trap; Listening to Space is Spiritual Wisdom.

- Third Eye Practices, such as *Mantra Chanting* and Affirmations can cause wandering with *karmic* ramifications that can continue for many lifetimes.

- When your wish becomes the cosmic wish, you become the cosmic channel.

Quantum Observer is the *Upanishadic* (उपनिषद्) *Brahma* (The God)

Quanto Mansi: It's an honour to interact with Quanto Shivo on *"Aham Brahmasmi*: Be the Cosmic Channel". Even though I have interacted with him many times, I am truly excited to interact with him on this theme. One of the beauties of interacting with Shivo is, even if we have interacted on the same topic the previous night, the next morning he has channelled something new and something current... So, I'm super excited for this.

Let me start with mentioning that Quantum scientists such as Heisenberg, Schrödinger, Bohr have been great fans of the *Upanishads* (उपनिषद्), of the *Vedanta*... and in fact Heisenberg famously said that so many ideas of quantum science seemed crazy to him until he came across the *Upanishads* (उपनिषद्) and *Vedanta*, and then they started to make any sense... *Upanishad* literally means sitting next to the master and receiving that channelling of his, today we are really honoured to sit next to Shivo, an enlightened master and receive the channelling...

Shivo, in the *Upanishads* (उपनिषद्), there are four *Mahāvākyas (the grand Sutras* (सूत्र), two of which are *Aham Brahmāsmi* and *Tat Tvam Asi* (*"तत् त्वम् असि"*). How would you explain them on the basis of Quantum Sciences?

Quanto Shivo: The *Upanishad Mahāvākyas* say I am God and so are you... let us understand in terms of science, what is God?... we have been told in scriptures that God is omnipresent, he is everywhere, he is formless and yet every form emanates from him... Hindu metaphysics describes God as the observer, the source of creation; when God awakens, the creation begins... Quantum sciences accord the highest place to the observer; it mentions that observation is the highest act of creation... after the discovery that universe is expanding, and that too at an accelerating pace, the Big Bang theory of creation has come under serious questioning, which Big Bang theorists are not able to resolve...

this has given rise to **the Quantum Theory of Creation**, which mentions that Cosmos got created with the awakening of Observer... surprisingly, this is exactly what Hindus have always mentioned, *Brahma* (the ever expanding God) awakened from slumber and creation began...Quantum scientists say that the subatomic particles, raw material of creation were always available, they sometimes call it **Quantum Foam;** as the observer awakened, it started to organize itself as matter... Hindus say, *Shakti* nudged *Shiva* out of his sleep, they got united and creation began...both the concepts are surprisingly similar...

I AM GOD: Merger of Cosmic and Personal Electro-Magnetic Fields

Quanto Shivo: Let me now explain God in scientific terms. God is the electromagnetic field that pervades all over the cosmos, scientists have discovered a faint electromagnetic field that not only pervades all over the cosmos, but beyond it... it can be said that the universe emanated from this field... this is exactly what the Hindu God is, all pervading and the source of cosmos... this is what we say, the God is all around us, as we are moving in the world we are moving in God, like the fish moving in water.

Now, what is *Aham?* the 'I'? What is the purest form of 'I'?... the soul, isn't it?... now, what is soul?... let me now refer to Einstein here, he said that every object is spatially extended, it means everything you see in a particular fixed place, at some kind of a time space co-ordinate, pervades all over the cosmos, it may physically exists at a specific location, but electromagnetic field of that pervades all over the cosmos... *Upanishads* उपनिषद्‌mention the same truth about our soul, that our soul pervades in the whole cosmos, our soul is everywhere... when we realise that nature of soul, the one which is omnipresent, that is when we come to know that, "I am God", *"Aham Brahmasmi"*. God pervades everywhere, it can also be explained as God is Space... hence, the realisation "I am God" is to experience yourself in space, in the omnipresent space... "I am God" means "I am space"... you begin to experience the oneness with space, like I am everywhere in space... this reminds me of a Bollywood Hindi song from the famous film, *"Ram Teri Ganga Maili"*: *"मुझको देखोगे जहाँ तक, मुझको पाओगे वहाँ तक, इस ज़मीं आसमाँ तक, मैं ही मैं हूँ, दूसरा कोई नहीं!"* *"mujhko dekhoge jahan tak, mujhko paoge wahan tak, is zameen se aasman tak, main hi main hu, dusra koi nahi"*, meaning: till wherever you can see, you will find me, from the earth till the sky, I am everywhere, there is no one else... it is truly amazing that this esoteric *sutra* सूत्र is also part of popular culture in India...

To this great *sutra* सूत्र, the another *sutra* सूत्र has also been added: *'Tat Tvam Asi'* (*"तत् त्वम् असि"*)... this serves a great purpose that 'I am God' don't become the statement of arrogance... this is for us to understand that not only I am God, but you are also God, everyone is God... *Aham Brahmasmi* is the truth, not just for me but for you also... If the second *sutra* सूत्र did not exist, *Aham Brahmasmi* would have become the state of ultimate ego, I am super powerful, I dominate. I am bigger than you... but that possibility is negated with the second *sutra* सूत्र *"Tat Tvam Asi"* *"तत् त्वम् असि"*, *"You too are so"*... "I am God and so are you"... so when you go into this space of soulfulness, you realize I am God and so is everyone.

Quanto Mansi: Shivo, you have mentioned this before too, if it's only the first वाक्य *(vākya)* (speech) *Aham Brahmasmi* and not the other, you would be like *Ravan* right? The peak of ego?... on the contrary, *Rama* was someone who realized the second महावाक्य उपनिषत् *(Mahāvākya)* too, which is why he was able to see the heroic in so many people like *Sita, Hanuman, Angad, Vibhishun*, even in *Jatayu, Kevat and Shabri*...

How We Fell from 'I am Soul' to 'I am Body'?

Quanto Mansi: Shivo, what you said is amazing in theory and concept, and probably in reality experienced by masters like you, but if this is so omnipresent, if it is everywhere then why aren't we all experiencing this? If this is the ultimate reality and we are like fish swimming in water, then why are we not experiencing this? Why do we come to the identification "I am Body", and fall from our peak realisation of *"I am soul"*; from *"I am space"* we got crunched into *"I am body"*, Why does that happen?

Quanto Shivo: Let us first distinguish the conscious state *"I am Space"* from the subconscious state of "I am Body"... According to "String Theory", everything in this world emanates from vibrations, similarly in spiritually too, whole world emanates from the causal body, the fourth body, which is nothing else but the vibrations... now, there are two kinds of vibrations, the concentrated vibration and the holistic vibration... holistic vibration is the one which doesn't have centre or even if it does have centre it is spread out in vast space, these vibrations move in an outward movement; the concentrated vibration is totally opposite to this, it has specific boundary, the vibrations move inwards towards the centre... holistic vibrations are conscious and concentrated vibrations are egoistic... the vibration of love is spread out everywhere, you will feel love everywhere, all over... On the contrary, all the negative vibrations, the subconscious vibrations like the fear, the greed, the revenge, the anger, hatred, are all concentrated, all these have specific boundaries... The divine vibrations, the conscious vibrations are holistic, omnipresent without boundary, and the subconscious ego vibrations are concentrated bounded vibrations... This is the essential distinction all spiritual seekers must know...

When you are living with the understanding *"I am Space"* and life is happening to you, you are fully present in that moment, you are living each and every moment as it happens to you... however, what if you are not fully present in this moment?... When you cannot just accept what is happening and you are wishing that the reality should have been different... If you are in such a state of being, in the state of non-acceptance of life, obviously you are not living that moment fully.

There was a huge phenomenon that negatively impacted the collective consciousness of humanity... we went through a long period of descending *yuga* युग... many of us would have known about the *yuga* युग cycle, these have been part of Hindu scriptures, and now there is immense astronomical and scientific evidences too that these cycles exist... these cycles are of approx. 24,000 years of duration, equally divided in descending and ascending phases, in ascending *yuga* युग

phase the consciousness moves up, and in descending *yuga* युग cycle the consciousness moves down… we have been going through the descending phase, and the very low conscious phase of *Kaliyuga* कलियुग… We began to feel the rise in consciousness from 18th century onwards, with the advent of *Dwapar Yuga* द्वापर युग, and now we are suddenly in the era of galactic transit, the zone of extremely high consciousness…

We were in Plasmic phase 12,000 years back too, but it was almost the peak of consciousness and from there, the consciousness began to descend, and with that, our sense of *"I am space"* constantly gets crunched and our understanding got limited to the material, the physical… it became very difficult to live the moment fully as the consciousness kept reducing, and life continuously became more and more difficult… we kept accumulating these unlived moments in our subconscious, through our life after life journey… all these unlived moments are accumulated in subconscious as concentrated vibrations, and manifesting in our body as well as aura… and the understanding of *"who am I?"* is now reduced just to the body or may be little bit of our aura… that is how we have gotten disconnected with a very natural state of *"Aham Brahmasmi,* I am God, I am soul, I am space".

Is Life Too Complicated or Too Simple?

Quanto Mansi: Shivo, this is really amazing… I want to help clarify this for everyone, how practical is this, so applicable in everyday life… so please correct me if I am wrong, but for example let's say, here I am in a forest camp in US, at below zero degrees Celsius, in an office somewhere trying to find Internet and when Khussal asked me to deliver a talk… I did want to do it, but then I also have to consider the current reality and then make a decision… so what I did was, I just checked into my body before I made that decision… can I just check both these choices in my body and see, if I'm saying yes or no to him…, where am I feeling both these choices in my body… maybe I'm anxious of how would I pull it off, and I was having a little anxiety in my heart, what if there is no Internet, what if I can't... I felt a little bit sweaty palms and after I observed in space and was guided to clarify a few things, I was completely at peace with it... is this a technique?... I mean it sounds so high *funda*, but it is a *sutra* सूत्र that we can check in our life... when you are faced with making a choice, or especially a tough choice, just check your body... where are you feeling it? Are you feeling sweaty? Are you feeling some sensations in any specific part of the body, some heat, some pain, some palpitation, some pressure, some numbness???... just check your body and observe the space... keep observing it and there'll be a time where you will feel these vibrations spreading out into the space, and then the vibrations move into your body and that's when you make a decision... Shivo, is that a practical takeaway of this?

Quanto Shivo: You've so beautifully described the whole process... Yes!!! It is very practical and I just recalled something... right now, we are having our 21 days' workshop on exactly the same subject *"Aham Brahmasmi - Be the Cosmic Channel"*!... there was a question or a comment, *"Isn't life too complicated?"*... for every choice you make, you have to consider so many things, so much opens up unexpectedly on the way, of which we were not aware while we made the choice, we have to delve into so much unknown, there are so many, just so many factors to consider... any choice you want to make between A and B, appears so very difficult.

Quanto Mansi: Yeah! And we have to keep making choices all the time... and how our life shapes up, is really the outcome of how good our choices have been... every choice is so complicated, and no wonder, life appears so complicated...

Quanto Shivo: There are so many considerations involved in a choice, you consider all the possible aspects, and yet we fail so often, still the choices go wrong... right???... Isn't life too complicated???... when we know this state of *"Aham Brahmasmi"*, life is just too simple, not just when you have reached the state of *"Aham Brahmasmi"*, but even when you begin to move towards it, even if you have taken just one step... as you become aware of the space around you, you would realise life is increasingly becoming simple... Why???, because everything you feel, whatever vast numbers of considerations are there. The only thing you need to do is, feel everything, feel the emotions attached to every choice, feel the vibrations of those emotions in your body and around your body... feel everyone who is involved, their emotions, their vibrations... feel everything in the space... that's it... Just become aware of the space... just become aware of the space... and as soon as you are aware of the space, you will know what is the right choice!... not only you will know the right choice, but you would find huge synchronicities along the way, because choice was not made by you, but by the cosmos... so not only have you made the right choice, but you have found all the support needed to execute that choice. This is the Cosmic Channeling!

Quanto Mansi: Yes, I have experienced this...

Seeding of New Vision and the Synchronicity Galore

Quanto Shivo: There are going to be blocks to whatever choice you make, there are obstacles all around... especially for the creative, unique choices, the futuristic choices, these are not yet part of mass consciousness, the collective subconscious of the world is going to fight this new beginning tooth and nail.... and that is when you realise the true power of synchronicities, every time you feel stuck, every time you tend to give up after total efforts, path will still open up for you.

That is the magic when cosmos makes choice, it takes charge of making it happen when you give up, it finds most unusual unpredictable, never before kind of ways for that seed to blossom, which has been sown by the cosmos and was channelled through you.... such kind of dawn of new vision happens when you felt the space and your emotion, consideration, everything dissolved into the space and the cosmic choice channeled through you.

It is not just that the choice has come to you but also the whole path of that choice keep opening up, it is the synchronicity galore... it is in this state of surrender to cosmos, you realise the truth of the saying, which is a belief for lot of us, that 'everything happens for good'... but you will realise the truth of this, that 'everything happens for good', only if you are aware of the space, you are grounded in the space... when you are grounded in the space everything that happens to you is for good.

Quanto Mansi: Yes Shivo, I've seen this, everything aligns up... It's like you've made the choice and somehow all the dots are lining up and everything is what it's meant to be, everything just lines up... this is how I feel, the conscious choice is even beyond the intelligent choices, which tend to fail quite often...

Follow Your Heart: The Superstition of New Age Spirituality

Quanto Mansi: Shivo, that brings me to another important point... many times, especially in the new age spiritual circles, we say *'follow your heart'*, listen to what heart is saying, listen to my inner voice, the God inside me who is saying this, 'Guru is within me', or some people say I just felt like this or this was my hunch or whatever... what do you think about that? Is that also coming from this space? Where is this coming from?

Quanto Shivo: These are the great superstitions of the new age spirituality: God is within me, follow my heart... it can only trap you into a mess very soon... let's understand why this happens...

Now it is a widely accepted fact that the subconscious is far bigger than the conscious in today's era... how big?... some scientists say that the subconscious is two thousand times bigger, some say it is twenty times bigger, but everybody agrees that in comparison to the subconscious, the conscious is just too little... so the voice you are hearing from the inside, is the voice of subconscious, that is not the voice of God... and if you follow that you are soon in mess.

Quanto Mansi: Shivo, you've already given us the *sutra* सूत्र for the conscious and the subconscious... if this is felt in one part of the body in concentrated form that is subconscious, if it is felt in a holistic way, all over, it is conscious... yeah!!!.

Listen to the Space, That is the Right Guidance

Quanto Shivo: God is not just within us, he is inside as well as outside, God is all pervasive... when you access God within as well as outside, that's when you have the right guidance... you need to transcend from the voice of heart to voice of Space... when you get the inner guidance, feel that, feel the emotions of that, feel the vibrations of that, feel the space around you and those vibrations... voice of heart then will dissolve and merge into the space and then the vibrations from space will rush in... this is what the right guidance is, the vibrations rushing into you from space carry the guidance of God...

Quanto Mansi: So Shivo, what you're saying is, let's say a person got angry, he was feeling it maybe in his face, his face got hot, his nose started flaring up... as he starts observing the space around that, it starts to dissolve and after a period of time as it dissolves there will be a new fresh vibration entering the face and the body, and that's the time to really make that decision to move forward... Wonderful!!!.

Mantra Chanting / Affirmations: The Spiritual Trap

Quanto Mansi: Shivo, I'm now entering into controversial territory... we know that, you've been a critic of third eye spiritual practices, such as affirmations and *mantras*... however, in past *mantras* have been channelled by the great sages, for e.g., *Markandeya Rishi* channelled the *Mahamrityunjaya Mantra*, *Vishvamitra Rishi* is credited with channelling the *Gayatri Mantra*... was that not channelling?...

Why can we not repeat those *mantras* for spiritual upliftment... also, why not to practice affirmations?... what is wrong in repeating, I am healthy, I am rich. I am this, that... they seem to work for many people... what is your take on that?... Do they work or do they not?... What are the consequences of that?... What is the *karma* related to that?... Can you please just delve into that???

Quanto Shivo: All kinds of *mantra* chanting, affirmations are the Third Eye practices, not the *Crown Chakra* practices... *Third Eye* is the crescendo of who you can be as identity, but for divinity, crescendo is reached at *Crown Chakra*... at third eye, you feel the concentration, the focus, and not the surrender or soul or omnipresence of God... in today's era people have started to believe that third eye practices are spiritual, but actually they are not... you just feel the eruption of energy with these practices... eruption of energy is not a spiritual experience, it is the merger and dissolution of energy into the space that takes you into spiritual realm... when people are not aware of this, third eye practices can often become a trap and lead you to wandering which may continue for many, many, life times, hence it is a major spiritual trap...

However, there was a time when these practices were helpful on a spiritual path, let me explain this in a bit of detail... In descending *yuga* युग the consciousness progressively reduced, the past was always better than the present and the future... hence, to move into the higher conscious state, you had to go back in the past... so, it was the spiritual wisdom to tap into the vibrational fields such as *mantras*, that were channelled by these great sages in the past, these would transport you into the state of higher consciousness... when the consciousness was continuously declining, these spiritual practices were much needed, these were the valid ways of becoming more conscious because the vibrations of past were more conscious.

Grounding in Space: The Ascending Yuga युग Spiritual Practice

Quanto Shivo: Now, we are in the ascending yuga युग, the consciousness is constantly rising, becoming higher than before, so the practices of tapping into the past are no more helpful... what is needed now is to become present in this moment... this does not mean, we discard the past, rather, we integrate it into the present moment, we acknowledge the past, learn from it, include it, and yet at the same time, don't get limited by the past... be in the present moment and know that in this present moment the past is also included... hence, the key is oneness with space, and not the mantra chanting... that is why if you see this grand *sutra* सूत्र of *Aham Brahmasmi* is the crescendo of उपनिषद् *Upanishads*, it is mentioned in so many *Upanishads* उपनिषद् in so many different ways... practice of mantra chanting is described in वेद: Vedas and not in *Upnishads* उपनिषद्... these peak *sutra* सूत्र of *Aham Brahmasmi* descended when the consciousness was very high, it descended in the Himalayan area, the space of peak consciousness...

In today's era, lot of people follow affirmations... many of them are able to manifest their desires too, but it is a spiritual trap... the problem is, through affirmations you are just focusing on one small part of the reality and one day, that major part of reality which you neglected, will sweep you away like a whirlpool... that is why, lot of people claim to manifest through affirmations, but what they don't realise, that either these are very unstable, or these turn out to be a trap in a way they could not imagine beforehand, or they have to face huge repercussions in other dimensions of life... they have to pay a very heavy cost of constantly demanding fulfilment of what they want because they are refusing to acknowledge what the life is, at this moment....

They are just whining like kids, "I want this, I want this, I want this" without even questioning if that is good for them... in their insistence, they are treating life as their adversary, they are believing that since life does not take care of them, so they have to demand what they want... can you see how immature and stupid it is?

Life has a platter full of possibilities, right in this moment, but you go on demanding the things, which may not be of much worth... wise people quickly realise that affirmations are a big trap and they quickly move away from such practices...

Download Your Own Gita

Quanto Mansi: Shivo, but the most beloved channelings, I would say the most known channelling that has happened in the world and in India, has been the *"Bhagavad Gita"*, so many famous people and gurus have rendered their commentaries on it... what is the crux of it for you? What is the essence that is relevant to us today?

Quanto Shivo: Essence is very clear: *to be present to the moment....* *Arjuna* is giving all the references of morality from past; he's quoting the morals written in the scriptures, he is clear that war is immoral... and what is *Krishna* saying?... he is so clearly distinguishing between good and bad *karma*, and it is not a moral distinction...

Krishna says, "Every karma we do under the influence of your ego, the l, your I-ness is a bad karma, it doesn't matter how good you think that karma is, but if it is emanating out of your ego it is a bad karma" ... and everything you do as guided by God is good *karma*... ... So the question is, how do you know the guidance of God?...

Obviously for that, you have to be in this moment, so *Krishna* is constantly saying be present in this moment... the spiritual practice he is suggesting is the *Sakshi Bhav*, the witnessing, which is again about being present in this moment... he is saying God is here right now, listen to him, listen to what he's saying and act in accordance with that... that is the message of *Gita*, to get grounded in space and channel, listen what God is saying right now, what God is guiding you through... That is Gita.

We may have so many conditions, so many social pressures, so many moralities, so many rights and wrongs... we may have so much knowledge about what is written in the scriptures, all that... consider all that, but don't get limited to that, listen to the moment...

This is what *Gita* is... and ironically, look at what we are doing, we are again following the *Gita* that was downloaded five thousand years back, that is irony... *Gita* has got very beautiful *sutras* सूत्र to learn from, to imbibe from, but that is not the whole reality of this moment... we have to download the reality of this moment, right at this moment... so *Gita* is something to learn from. It is a very beautiful scripture, but that is not something to be followed word by word... what we need to follow is, what is the guidance which is coming to you from space right at this moment?

Quanto Mansi: Shivo, this is really mind-blowing... like, am I supposed to download my own *Gita*, like, this is like, it is like, totally you know???

Quanto Shivo: This is the ascending *yuga* युग, unfortunately, in the name of spirituality whatever practices we follow, they all have come from, at least most of them, or almost all of them have come from descending *yuga* युग, from the past… ascending *yuga* युग practice is to download your own *Gita*, to feel your own *Gita* right now, to get guided from space… that is the guidance you need to receive, and that is the most potent spiritual practice of our times.

Let Your Wish Be the Cosmic Wish

Quanto Mansi: Shivo, I am going to ask, uhhh! maybe a child-like question… You said about following the wish of God, right? What about my wish? Uhhh…, You know what about my wish? What about my longing? What about that?

Quanto Shivo: Such kind of contradictions arise, when there is a lack of trust in life… when we trust life, we know that life takes care of all our wishes, if a wish has come to you, you should know that it is the wish of life, that you wish that… so life takes care, always… the problem is, you have a certain way in which your wish should be fulfilled… and that is where the problem is, this is what makes you try hard, you make plans and strategies, but then you finally realise you are a failure, even if your wish is fulfilled….

What if you could just offer your wish to God… say to him, "God this is the wish I have, and it is you who have sent this wish to me, so you show me the way"… and God will show you the way to fulfil your wish… and not just that, just know whatever is your wish, that's what the cosmos is wishing for you… just respect your wish, long for it, because the deep truth is that what I am living, my wish, my desire is not just my desire, but it is the desire of the whole cosmos for me… live it like cosmos is living through me and you will be surprised… God takes care of everything you wish.

Quanto Mansi: Shivo, I am feeling so inspired by what you said… you know, I'm feeling that we are so limited, our dreams, our wishes also will be limited… Now if we let God, who is so unlimited, who is so omnipresent, if he dreams for us, he wishes for us, how grand that could be, right?

Quanto Shivo: Yeah!!!, the big mistake is, we think that I know best, what is good for me... SORRY!!!, you don't know! whatever you may know, is going to trap you very soon... God knows!... see, the way you have plans for yourself, God has plans for you, and those plans are far grander, and are far wiser... so if there is a conflict between "the plan I have for myself and the plan God has for me", always choose "the plan God has for you"... that is the Cosmic Channelling... when you live by the wish of God, that is the Cosmic Channelling.

Quanto Mansi: As we conclude, uhhh!!! I have to say that I have seen Shivo live this... I've seen him live that this is my wish, but this is the wish of God and I am going to trust it...

And that is why he is my Guru...

So, Shivo, thank you so much for this interaction!

DAY - 1

TRUTH OF THE MOMENT

- *Sutra* that makes your life simple in the current era of chaos: Acknowledge this moment, and your struggle will vanish.

- Meeting of paradoxes leads to the Quantum leap.

- Connect to the Collective Vibrational Field for an accelerated evolution and *Karma* cleansing.

- Collective observation is so potent that it can even liberate wandering entities.

- Total trust means total surrender, with no expectations.

- Spiritual journey happens not just within you but also outside of you.

- Feel the entire "scatteredness", all at the same time, in totality, and you will become the master of the situation

- Something that got created here, will last for the next 100 years to come.

- Observation cleanses not just what we are aware of, but even the next layer, of which we were not aware.

- Solidity of the body is an illusion, when you become aware of it's porosity, the inner and outer space meet and merge.

- Space is buzzing with sensuous experiences like sound, light, touch, smell and taste.

- Connect with space when spirituality, etc. seems unbelievably useless.

- If you can experience variation in space, you get attuned with the cosmos and begin to channel.

- Comparisons with past moments is taking you away from the beauty of this very moment.

- Feel any group, the family, the office, etc. in space and you start to become it's guide, pioneer, leader.

- When you look at everything inside the Space, your relationship with the world will get uplifted.

- If you acknowledge the truth of this moment, moment after moment, you will begin to get glimpses of *Aham Brahmasmi.*

Participants of this workshop have been keenly waiting for this workshop to being. There is huge anticipation in air. Everyone is waiting to know how do we begin on this journey. And what gets revealed is the most vital sutra on this journey: Truth of This Moment. Each time you acknowledge the Truth of This Moment, and surrender it to cosmos, you will have the glimpse of divinity. If you can just keep living the Truth of This Moment, continuously, moment after moment, you will keep moving towards the ultimate truth, the ultimate reality: Aham Brahmasmi. Every other spiritual practice, be it Worship, Breathing, Fasting, Mantra Chanting, Affirmation, Visualization, Concentration, Recitation, is secondary to this understanding: Truth of This Moment. Day 1 interaction is about exploring the multiple dimensions of Truth of Moment, which includes not just your own truth, but also the truth of others involved in a specific situation, and how observation and surrender provides not just the glimpse of ultimate reality but also the mastery in worldly situations.

Truth of This Moment; Let Your Struggle Vanish

Quanto Shivo: I am inviting everyone to feel, to acknowledge what is this moment for you? Maybe just with one sentence, at most two sentences and as you say that, feel that in your body, in your aura; and when others are sharing their acknowledgement, feel that too... and you will feel that in space too, because it is coming from somewhere else to you. When you are able to feel what others are saying it gets easier for you to feel the space... I hope everyone got that!

Jeet: I feel depth right now, that's all I can say! I feel depth, like going deep... It is depth not death! It is not really a sinking feeling, because sinking is different. This feels like going deeper almost like we do grounding but in a slightly different way.

Quanto Shivo: Rooting, in one word.

Jeet: Yes!

Raghu: Acknowledging my position or acknowledging people's position? Can you please explain?

Quanto Mansi: This moment Raghu, whatever this moment means for you, and in includes what you feel, as well as what other people feel.

Quanto Shivo: Yes! What is this moment like for you, Raghu??? This is the most vital art to learn for all spiritual seekers: "To acknowledge this moment!" This simple *sutra* can resolve much of your struggle. If we can just learn to acknowledge this moment, you will see that your struggle will simply vanish, okay? Let's say, if someone is throwing his anger on you, if you can just acknowledge that this person is angry and I am feeling suffocated, you will see the sudden shift right at this moment.

Rajkkumarii: I am feeling very peaceful.

Kawal: Feeling very still!!!! Not just stillness, but excitement too.

Quanto Shivo: Very good!!! If you are still and yet excited, both at the same time, this is the meeting of paradoxes... when the paradoxes meet, that is always the time of leap.

Rucchi: What I feel is... uhhhh!!! I have been feeling like the Death Card in the Tarot Deck. Past two days have been really like a roller coaster ride, this is what I feel in the moment. It just, just now happened, I was doing this tarot reading, Mansi asked, "Are you doing this programme?" I didn't even read what it was! It was like a leap of faith; it just came as a default YES! So I'm feeling the simplicity of the universe... the universe gives clues, we just need to accept, so I'm just feeling, it is so simple.

Quanto Shivo: Thank you Rucchi! Very deep expression of the truth of the moment, you included multiple dimensions of this moment.

Jyotsna: At this point of time, I'm feeling very much excited and intensely receptive.

Creation of Collective Vibrational Field

Quanto Shivo: Is everyone feeling, what everyone is acknowledging as their truth of this moment? We are experiencing the creation of a collective vibrational field of this workshop, which will turn this journey of 21 days, not just the individual journey happening together, but the collective journey that will impact each one of us individually. This is the *sutra* for *accelerated karma* cleansing, individual as well as collective.

Anonymous 1: I feel fear and quite emotional right now... there is a dip in my heart!!!

Ajay: I'm feeling blank right now.

Quanto Shivo: Wonderful!!!

Suman: Same here... I also feel blank, and emptiness inside me. I feel nothing is there.

Quanto Shivo: Okay! Thank you! Can we just be present to this being blank? Being blank is a wonderful stage.. It's like an empty cup, totally receptive. Though, on the opposite side, it could also be kind of a desperation that I don't understand anything. Just be present to whatever it is.

Latha: I'm just feeling a sense of helplessness... and also a sense of deep trust and faith.

Trust is Total Surrender, With No Expectations

Aruna: I'm feeling full.

Quanto Shivo: You're feeling full???

Aruna: Yes. I'm feeling, as if everything is till the brim of the glass, like It's just going to be pukish or something.

Quanto Shivo: Oh! Okay!... So, something is emerging from inside you?

Aruna: I don't know... It's very repulsive also.

Quanto Shivo: Just be present to this.

Aruna: Okay Sir!

Quanto Shivo: Maybe something is just being forced out, because of your own observation, as well as the consciousness of this space, the collective observation.

Aruna: Like it's coming till my throat, it's like someone is holding my neck, and like I'm not going to live.

Quanto Shivo: Just be present to, I'm not going to live, and trust... just trust.

Aruna: Okay!

Quanto Shivo: And trust is not, that I will live, that's not the real trust! It is a kind of trust, but that's not the peak of the trust. Peak of the trust is, even if I don't live it is fine... I'm thankful! I live or don't live yet I'm thankful!

Aruna: Right!!!

Quanto Shivo: Can you be in that space???

Aruna: Yes! There is a lot of palpitation.

Quanto Shivo: Can you live in gratitude??? in thankfulness???... in such acceptance that even if I die it's alright! So Aruna, Are you ready to trust that even if you die, it is a blessing? Are you ready to trust???

Aruna: Uhhh!!! I'm unable to surrender also.

Quanto Shivo: Yeah!!! So, if you're unable to surrender, just be present to this too. Yeah, who else???

Jyoti: I'm feeling total surrender.

Power of Authentic Sharing

Sakha: Entering here, coming into this space felt very blessed... I am feeling as if my body has melted and as if the soul is flying in the air, I don't know, feeling bodyless.

Quanto Shivo: Thank you! and as you shared this, now we all can feel that too! This is the power of collective vibrational fields. Anyone shares any beautiful experience, it will be rubbed on to you and if you share anything difficult, that will begin to evaporate quickly, because of the collective observation. This is how everyone can support everyone, just by way of authentic sharing. A spiritual journey is not just an individual journey, it is not just about going in, it is within you as well as outside you, both the dimensions.

Vaibhav: Sir, I'm feeling blank and open, receptive.

Vyjayanti: Shivo! I am feeling a lot of palpitation in my heart... at the same time a feeling of being very silent, just be very quiet.

Divya: I'm feeling sceptical... I'm also feeling trust... also confused...

Atin: Shivo sir! I'm feeling very much a part of *Shiva*, and I'm feeling that I am on the gate of *Shiva* dimension... and I'm starting off my spiritual journey with this programme.

Quanto Mansi: I'm feeling, I'm actually feeling like uhhhh!!! It's exactly how it is supposed to be, that really everything is just exactly how it needs to be right now.

Rohini: I'm not sure... I'm feeling nervous, I don't know why??? Lots of chaos, but at the same time I'm trying to pull myself together, but I don't know!!! there is a lot happening in the stomach.

Quanto Shivo: Okay thank you!!! Is everyone sitting straight in the *Quanto Asana*??? Just sit straight. This is the best way to feel the whole and even to feel ourselves. Anyone else???

Neelam: Feeling a lot of palpitation in my heart, uhhh!!! restless and tired!

Observation Resolves Worldly Conflicts

Manisha: I am listening because I'm in the market and just now I came back... I'm just listening.

Quanto Shivo: Manisha can you acknowledge this moment? See this is a great art in life... let's say Manisha was in the market, she just came and she's feeling, Oh!!! The programme has started! Can you acknowledge this moment Manisha???, it is a miracle to be in this moment... the moment you acknowledge this moment, the truth of this moment, see what happens to you!... What is the truth of this moment???

Manisha: Shivo sir! Actually when I just entered, and you were asking everyone to acknowledge this moment, there was an argument, there was a fight, I was getting angry... and I want to share, when you were just speaking, I felt that you were saying that for me. 5-6 days back something happened that was literally the *Tower moment* for me, something happened between me and my husband and when he was scolding, and I was just feeling this in my body. If it was the Manisha from before, I would have rebelled, but instead I experienced it fully... and after one hour I saw my husband's anger settling down, and we were just like before as if nothing had happened... It was like WOW!!!, the power of observation.

Quanto Shivo: Thank you!!! Yes! that is the power of observation... So what do you observe, what is this moment?... how is the reality appearing to you right now???... what is the truth of this moment???

Manisha: Frankly speaking Shivo sir, from the last 2 years whatever you and Mansi are teaching us, I am flowing with this totally... my life problems have become very less, incidents like these don't perturb, because let go happens easily... this is what I am feeling, yes, I am feeling more blissful day by day...

Quanto Shivo: Thank you!!!

Making Empowering Choices, Even If Your Life is Scattered

Rashi: Shivo, I'm feeling scattered... and I'm feeling everywhere, that I'm here, there, everywhere.

Quanto Shivo: This is not everywhere, like *Aham Brahmasmi*, right? Ha Ha Ha (laughs)

Rashi: No No!!! It's like I'm feeling scattered.

Quanto Shivo: Yeah!!! Can you see the point???... the beauty is, if you can feel the whole of the scatteredness all at the same time, you will suddenly feel the mastery of the whole situation... the whole situation will get integrated, it will become one... the point is, you are feeling the scatteredness of various multiple components one by one, so you are feeling the situation partially at any point, and that is why it is troubling you. Now! instead of feeling it one by one, feel all the components of scatteredness as one. The moment you can feel the whole scatteredness at the same time, you will suddenly know you are the master and will know what to do.

Rashi: Okay!!!

Quanto Shivo: Can you just feel everything that is making you feel scattered???... just feel everything! This is one great *sutra* for everyone If you're feeling split... if you're feeling this! and that! and that! you feel nervous, you feel anxious, you feel overwhelmed, you feel the burden of the whole situation... you are bound to make mistakes when you are in this state. But, if you just close your eyes, feel everything, all at once, everything becomes part of one whole and suddenly you have the mastery.

Nishtha: I'm also feeling, being all over the place, very scattered... and uhhhh!!! This is the moment I want to run away from...

Quanto Shivo: When you feel scattered, it is because you're feeling partial.... whatever is making you feel scattered, just be present to everything all at the same time. And this is the *sutra* of mastery.

Nishtha: It's very uncomfortable.

Quanto Shivo: Just close your eyes... keep remembering, I'm feeling scattered about this, about that... acknowledge those 10 fragments... see how the mastery emerges... see how everything becomes clear to you and see how you are able to make the empowering choice, that will dissolve something. You're getting it?

Nishtha: Yes!!!

Kshitij: <u>Since the session has started, I'm just crying and crying and crying... I got a sentence in between, that something will get created here, which will last for 100 years.</u>

Quanto Shivo: Thank you!!!

Quanto Mansi: Shivo! You also share what is your state?

Quanto Shivo: Okay!... So what I am feeling is, whoever has shared whatever, has turned collective. It's like everything was going in some kind of a pool, okay???... that mixture has not become harmonious yet, but it is all together, so can everyone feel this presence all around you?

Sutra for Accelerated *Karma* Cleansing

Quanto Shivo: I invite everyone to close your eyes and feel the energy of this moment... the key for living in the moment is to acknowledge what is this moment???, this is what brings you back to the present moment... I invite everyone to acknowledge, what is this moment for you?... when you acknowledge this moment, feel it, feel it in your body, feel it in your aura... and also when everyone is acknowledging their own moment, feel their acknowledgement too, because whatever you are feeling is not the whole truth...

Feeling the acknowledgment of multiple sources gives you access to collective vibrational fields, and then even that begins to cleanse up, which you have no awareness about, which you have not even acknowledged... this is important, because if our observation could only cleanse what we are aware of, then only very little cleansing is possible. This is why it is important not just to acknowledge your own moment of truth, but also to be fully present to the moment of truth shared by everyone else too...

Even if the acknowledgements of this group of 30 people together, does not constitute the whole truth, there is something beautiful about such multiple acknowledgements... let's say if you acknowledge one event of your life, and you then acknowledge another event too, of similar nature; you know what, you have acknowledged not just these two events but also many more similar events before that, even the events, that are not in your awareness... if you acknowledge a pattern in this life, and you could also see the same pattern in your past life, observation will cleanse not just these two lives, but the similar patterns in many more lives before, even if you have no memory of that... this is the *sutra* for quick, accelerated *Karma* cleansing, this is the power of multiple acknowledgements, the cleansing spirals much deeper...

Similarly, let's say, if three people share their observation of any situation in a team meeting... the collective truth that has been acknowledged goes beyond what they have shared... here, we have almost 30 people sharing authentically their own acknowledgement of this moment... the combined effect of that is not 1 multiplied by 30, but it is something like 1 multiplied by 100 or 500, okay?... So, let's feel our own acknowledgment and let's feel the acknowledgment of everyone else too, okay?

Process for Collective Awareness and Observation

Please sit down in Quanto *Mudra* and Quanto *Asana*.

Feel everyone's sharing, it feels like pressure around you, around your body

Can you feel something coming from outside of you? These are the collective subconscious vibrations, and obviously feel heavy... Are you feeling that heaviness?

And now observe your breathing... Just let it go deep... do not manipulate your breathing, don't try to change it... just be in observation... and just with the observation, breathing changes by itself... be in observation of this too... I will not speak for the next two or three minutes, we will just observe our breathing. (Silence...)

Keep feeling that heaviness around you along with the breathing... observe both at the same time, the heaviness of the space and the breathing.

If your body is vibrating just experience that. Be with that

Feel the space around you... is the space touching you? There is a space inside your body and there is space outside your body. Are these two different spaces? Or is there some kind of porous state where inner space and outer space are merging into one as well?

It's an illusion that our body is solid... even in the atom 99.99 percent is space, so what appears as the solid body is actually space. Can you experience that?

Inner space and outer space are melting into one. Is there some kind of light in this space? Is the space buzzing with some kind of sound? Is there some kind of smell in the space? Is the space touching you? Can you taste the space inside your mouth? Experience the space around you and within you, with the five senses.

Keep breathing deeper... As you feel the porosity of your body, hidden vibrations just begin to erupt and flow outward

And around this collective space of the participants, is surrounded by the vast space, become aware of that... as soon as you become aware of that the heaviness of this space begins to dissolve.... if that heaviness is becoming lighter acknowledge that... and if it is not becoming lighter then acknowledge that too.

Just go in some kind of relaxation or shavasan. Take support of a wall. Just let go of yourself. I will now go silent for 2-3 minutes.

Did you feel the vibrations moving out, and can you now feel those coming in now?... this is the experience of us getting filled, the emptiness getting filled by the cosmic vibrations. These are the holistic vibrations that are coming in.

If you feel like breathing out from the mouth let it be so.

Feel the taste that is coming in your mouth. That is the taste of collective vibrations. You can feel a lot of magnetism around your tongue and around your body.

Can you feel how far this heaviness in space is? Can you feel that this heaviness becomes lighter and lighter.

Okay we can now open our eyes. Just be thankful for this experience of observation and awareness.

Collective Observation is Hugely Transformational

Quanto Shivo: Anyone wants to share any experience or insights received from this process?

Vyjayanti: Shivo, I felt that the outside was lighter and the inside was heavier. And slowly I started to feel like my lungs were trying to open up. Like my breathing tried to go deeper. Yeah that was the experience I had.

Quanto Shivo: This is because you could feel your aura and suddenly there is more opening in terms of breath. Yeah? thank you.

Kawal: I couldn't breathe initially. My mind was very restless so it was just going haywire and then after a certain time like there was so much heat coming out of my body. For a second, I went deep and then my mind took over again.

Quanto Shivo: Okay. Thank you.

Latha: I felt my inside and outside, my whole body porous. Uh, but all along my *crown chakra* was throbbing, and my whole body, there was a lot of vibration I could feel. So initially it is like my inside was very heavy and I think very slowly, towards the end, I felt slightly lighter. But it was like the whole throbbing of my crown and body.

Quanto Shivo: Okay. Thank you.

Suman: For me it was out of body experience because while you were telling to feel the breath, I felt like I am not breathing only. Earlier, I felt the heaviness. When you said space, it was like a very compact form and it was touching the whole of the body. Later on, I felt the ground that something is entering from there. And then I felt the vibrations on my right side, and rest of the body I didn't feel anything exists or not also. Few seconds before you said to taste or what you are tasting, I had a taste of very uhh, a strong thing. I don't remember the taste but it was very strong. And after getting up from the shavasana, I feel a sense of expansion.

Quanto Shivo: So yeah! when I said taste, it was when I actually felt that there was a taste in the collective aura. So, some of you might have felt the taste before I said it.

Suman: Yes, just a few seconds before you said so... and a sense of expansion yeah so it was very powerful. Thank you.

Aruna: Shivo sir, it is now very light and very beautiful but when it all began it was very heavy, very traumatic, very trembling and painful.

Pain in the whole body, in the heart, in the mind in my third eye chakra. Uhh... it was like each of my nerves was exactly in pain. But it actually got dissolved eventually, meaning I could feel that every moment was like I'm releasing something.

Quanto Shivo: Yeah so, I'm feeling that there is some liberation... and you were not releasing, it was getting released with the blessing of space.

Aruna: Yes, yes.

Quanto Shivo: I am also sensing the release of heaviness, many would have felt it... I am feeling there is liberation.

Aruna: But I could see many other things also. Like I could see many faces. Then I felt something like *Mahakali* took over me. My tongue, everything was like someone took the charge of releasing it.

Quanto Shivo: Okay. Thank you. Who else wants to share?

Jyotsna: Me Shivo! Actually, I felt very nauseous during the process and even after completion of that process I'm feeling very much nauseous.

Quanto Shivo: Okay! So, something is releasing. Are you getting a sense of that? That something from inside is coming out?

Jyotsna: Yes. Yes.

Quanto Shivo: Okay! wonderful. Thank you. Yes.

Rajkkumarii: When we started, I felt I was seeing Lord Shiva himself with the three lines. The whole forehead I could see. Then I could see the Trishul and then white light and golden light. I didn't feel like I'm in the body. It was like I'm totally out. I couldn't feel my body also and when you asked us to come back I literally had to force myself to come back because I didn't want to come back. It was like I was totally blank, I couldn't see my hand I couldn't see my body, I could see nothing except the light, the golden light. Meaning I was not here only, it was like that. Totally above in the cosmic space like.

Quanto Shivo: Thank you Rajkkumarii.

Rajkkumarii: Thank you sir. Thank you so much. It's beautiful and still vibrating like I want to keep my eyes closed and go back to that state.

Quanto Shivo: Okay. Thank you. Yes, anyone else wants to share? You can also share if you received any insight out of this.

Jyoti: *Pranaam* Shivo sir but now I'm feeling vibration throughout the body and heaviness on my *heart chakra*.

Quanto Shivo: Yeah so something wants to release Jyoti. Just allow. Just keep feeling it. Don't try to suppress it. Don't try to change it. Don't try to negate it. Don't try to deny it. Just feel what's happening. Just the acknowledgment of this moment.

Jyoti: Yeah! I saw the light then *Lord Krishna* also. Like there was bright light. I felt like *Lord Krishna* was there.

Quanto Shivo: Okay thank you Jyoti.

Vaibhav: Sir, first I was feeling imprints. Then when I started focusing on my breath, uh… like observing my breath after that I kept on sleeping. Then I slept while sitting and I kept on sleeping. I just woke up.

Quanto Shivo: So good, nice, you had a nice relaxation. Okay. Thank you.

Anonymous: Shivo, Pranaam. Primarily what has happened is my son has been down with 104 degrees F fever, I had asked you all to pray the other day. Now my husband also has suddenly started shivering with 103 degrees F fever, due to which I joined the session late. Now I have been listening to the experiences.

Quanto Shivo: Can you acknowledge this moment? Today what we discussed: what happens when we acknowledge the truth of this moment. So, what is the truth of this moment for you? What all you're feeling, what is the truth right now for you?

Spirituality is Useless, I can't Bear This

Anonymous: Shivo, very frankly just the other day 13th Jan is the day of my younger son passing. I just realised it was 12 years. On the same date, my elder son started getting a fever and it has continued till today. I was told to hospitalise him in the morning, yet against the doctor's advice I've got him home because I treat him with homeopathy also. I don't like to go to hospitals with this kind of thing. That whole thing in the morning, three to four hours, I was absolutely tense and at that time I was thinking I don't want to do any meditation, I don't want to do anything as long as my son is unwell, that was exactly how helpless I had felt at that time when he passed away. I used to do meditation at that time also. I used to focus on good things, prayer and all that. But when all this comes at that time I'm like God I can't do anything here. What matters to me at this moment is my son. This meditation, this spirituality or whatever is there I don't know, like nothing was coming to me.

Quanto Shivo: It was useless. It all feels useless.

Anonymous: Yes. It was like I just thought where 12 years have gone, I don't know, I felt uncomfortable.

Quanto Shivo: So, is this the truth of the moment for you? That you are questioning that you are praying, but what does it mean? It's meaningless! Is this the truth of the moment for you?

Anonymous: That was the truth of the moment till I came home and then like the x-ray came normal and my homoeopath again reassured me, that is why I joined in now. Just now when I was just going to join my husband came and he was shivering. So, I had decided that when all my work is done and I have given my son his medicine I will have it finished by 9 pm so I can join you all at 9.30 pm. Meanwhile, my husband came and I had to look after him and all that. So, I was thinking to myself at that time, that when all this happens, nothing, nothing at all matters. Like, this spirituality or all this, nothing matters. I'm completely in that moment like, God, please save this, I can't bear this.

Quanto Shivo: So, can you be with this truth that I can't bear this, this is all useless. All this means nothing to me. Can you just be with this? Can you just acknowledge that this is the truth for you at this moment? No morals, no spirituality, no high thinking, this is the truth of the moment for you. Can you just be with this? Can you just be present to this?

(**Quanto Shivo** closes his eyes and goes in silence.)

Quanto Shivo: And as she is feeling this, can everyone feel that suddenly the space has changed. Can everyone feel that? Let's just close our eyes and be with this. (Silence)

I'm hearing a lot of sounds in the space right now. (Silence)

Yes we can open our eyes. Uh yeah please continue with your sharing and if you had any experience right now.

Observation Shifts the Space Vibrations

Jaya: *Pranaam*, Shivo. There were three different spurts that I experienced. When we started the meditation, we were asked to be in a happy state of mind and then focus on our breathing. At that time, I felt there was a lot of anxiety in the space here, I could sense that. So that happiness was not blossoming. And uh... when you mentioned about, you know, the porosity of the body I could sense as if my tongue had got in the centre some splits uh and there was a kind of an acidic bitter kind of a taste, uh, that emerged. Uh, I don't know if it was bitter but it felt as if it was bitter. But I could sense a lot of hollowness in the body. And the third spurt was when I felt as if I'm nobody, I'm nothing, what am I, not even a molecule, not even an atom, nothing. A sense of nothingness came. So, this was my experience.

Quanto Shivo: Okay. Thank you. So, I hope that many of us could sense how the space changes... One person shares and something comes into observation, and you can actually experience that the space changes. And if you can experience that change in space that's what gives you mastery. And actually, that's what helps you become the cosmic channel. If you can experience this variation in space, that's what attunes you with the cosmos and that's how whatever space you are sensing, experiencing, you begin to channel for that space. You begin to channel that space.

Rohini: So, when we started I was acknowledging the feeling that I was running around, I wanted all tasks to finish so that I can sit down. While Akash (husband) was in the office and I am here, I was feeling what is running in Akash's mind, that chaos I could feel at the same time. I was also feeling, that I am able to join but Akash can't. And then suddenly something else came up, I got this pain in the right side of my chest. Very heavy pain suddenly and some taste also came. I could feel that taste on the tip of my tongue and within a few seconds I could feel some heaviness in my palm. I don't know what that was. And something was revolving, and it was heavy also. It was a kind of vibration or something I don't know. It was leaving or entering my body. I was feeling this revolving kind of thing from yesterday night. I don't know what is happening! And now you asked us to feel that heaviness, that pain got shifted from the right side of the chest to the left side and that pain has got dissolved. Where it went away I didn't come to know.

Quanto Shivo: So, something has left. Yeah! Thank you.

This Moment is Unique; Drop the Comparison with Any Past Moment

Anonymous: Shivo, I've not been able to sense anything shift in space. Uhh... the only thing I just wanted to share a little bit of is, when I was in the hospital today with the doctors that time it felt right now my focus is so much, on this body, body, body. And just now, when I came home, I thought my son is better, a little better than what it was, fever is not there. I have taken so many things for granted and everything is disarray or chaos or mess. But if every day I enjoy, then, probably, that would make more sense. I should invest more in my body, so that every moment I enjoy, because these moments have kind of spoiled everything, and when everything is moving nicely I should be grateful for the normal way of life because I am always unhappy, that this is not happening in my office, that is not happening, that is not there, etc. Today, it is, like, let office or anything go to hell, it makes no difference, as long as this beautiful body and my son is fine. This all was going on in my mind.

Quanto Shivo: This is the truth of the moment for you. Let's learn to live in the moment. This is the truth of this moment. Why compare with what happened before? What were you thinking? See this is just taking away, taking you away from this moment and your mastery is when you are in this moment. That's when you channel. That's when you are a channel when you can acknowledge the truth of this moment. Right? Not to compare it with the past. Not to compare how it could be in future. Just be in the present.

Quanto Mansi: Yeah, Shivo in the beginning I felt a lot of people, not people but I felt a lot of things. Uh… and I could feel, I could feel the energy coming in, I could feel the vibrations coming in, but towards the end, I felt the invocation continued even after you told everyone to come back and when everyone was sharing it, I felt the invocation was still continuing. Like, uh.., you know, I was getting connected even deeper to their experience and for me the invocation was continuing. And in the end, uh.., like, the whole space, uh…, it felt like a womb.

Quanto Shivo: Yeah!

Quanto Mansi: And I felt patient, at first. it felt like I am pregnant and then the space started feeling very pregnant and that's how it's feeling to me right now too.

Process for Cultivating Space Awareness

Quanto Shivo: Yeah. Okay. Thank you…, so, I will share one insight and one meditation practice and I will take another five minutes and then we'll close. So, the insight is about group work, so all of us are involved in various group situations, it could be a group called family, it could be a group called office, it could even be a group called crowd or whatever. Okay? So, if you can feel the group in the space that's when your mastery begins. If you felt this group in space and you could feel that there were suddenly so many releases. You became the master. Same way, you will see that you are in a situation, the situation is very difficult, and you can begin to feel that in space, suddenly, you will begin to feel that you are getting the right insight, you are getting the situation, you are getting the right plan of action, that is your mastery. So, this is the insight of today's experience.

And one meditation technique I would like you to experience tomorrow throughout the day is to experience the space. So, when we, let's say, look at the room, what do you see? You see things. Look outside the room, what do you see? You see the road and the houses and the trees and so on. Actually, everything exists in space. The moment you begin to see the space, how you look at everything will change. You look at the flower but look at the flower and the space around it. In fact, look at the space and inside that space there is a flower, right? Look at the space in the room and inside that space there is something. So, learn to look at space and the world inside it. Normally we are neglecting the space. So, when you learn to see the space as the context for everything that is when you begin to connect with the space. Also, just whenever you get an opportunity, look at the sky, go outside your room there is a lot of space.

I invite you to connect with space as much as possible. Okay? And, for tonight again, I would like you to continue with what we did right now, that is, to acknowledge the truth of this moment. This is something you can practise all your life, acknowledge the truth of this moment and that is the crux of Aham Brahmasmi.

If you can live life like that all the time, acknowledging the truth of this moment and to acknowledge how the past is coming into it, how the future is coming into it, and it is okay if the past and future is coming. But if that shifts you away from this moment, that is where the issue is. Okay, if the past comes into it, future comes into it, it's okay but that doesn't mean that you will get shifted into the past or future, okay?

So, acknowledge the truth of this moment and remain grounded in that truth. This is the key *sutra* for *Aham Brahmasmi.*

Thank you everyone for joining. Feel the space before you go to bed. Acknowledge the truth of the moment and go to sleep. Thank you very much!

(Shivo is with folded hands as *namaste*). *Shubhratri*! Goodnight!

DAY - 8

RESOLVING THE ISSUES OF VARIOUS CHAKRAS

- *Chakras* are not just inside the body, but also extended in space, this projects your inner conditioning in the outer world.

- *Solar Plexus* is the most active *chakra* in the current era of Ascending Dwapar.

- Alexander, the crescendo of *Solar plexus* conditioning, died desperate, empty handed and dissatisfied.

- Diogenes, the naked mystic of Greece, unnerved Alexander, made him feel how futile his life is.

- *Solar plexus* person often get trapped into disastrous unreal strategies.

- *Krishna* was grounded in heart, so he created many heroes.

- heart centric Lakshmi woman makes her man greatly successful.

- Contentment, the often quoted moral of the salaried class, is hollow if it is accompanied by contempt for the rich and successful.

- Sign of *Vishuddhi chakra* activation: presence of talented/capable people inspire you and not threaten you.

- Good girls who often sacrifice to gain approval, often get trapped in life.

- *Crown chakra* makes you long to become one and flow with life, while the *Third eye* is about will and determination.

- Trust in life is not about positive interpretations, but being ready for whatever comes up, because everything happens for good.

Chakras are the storehouse of conditioning and patterns in the second body, which is known as the Energy Body or Subtle body. As the seeker progresses this conditioning dissolves, and the experience of Chakras becomes less and less prominent. When one reaches the state of Aham Brahmasmi, all chakras merge into one and it's experience becomes miniscule. There exists an immense confusion about Chakras in spiritual circles, many seekers get misguided into believing that experiencing chakras is a spiritual experience, and hence they become attached with it. As they long for more intense Chakra experience, it becomes a block for the peak spiritual experience. The truth is that Chakra is an entry into the stored energy within you, and the spiritual experience happens when this energy dissolves into the space / consciousness. When one becomes the observer of chakras, the chakra conditionings. stored patterns and energy begin to dissolve into the soul, leading one to the glimpse of Aham Brahmasmi. Interaction of Day 8 is about how to become sensitive about your own chakra energy structures, the conditioning it has created, the worldly events it attracts, it's fulfilment on a specific chakra and moving up to the next one, and the most important how it;s obsevation leads to dissolution of idenity and the glimpse of Aham Brahmasmi.

Anonymous : I would like to give feedback that I feel much better than the other day... There will be ups and downs yes, but I feel much better physically and mentally.

Quanto Shivo: Happy to know this!!!

Your *Chakras*, Extended into Space, Bridge the World

Let's connect with the space... let's see if something is automatically coming up for us or space wants to convey something through us... just close your eyes... go in deep.

If you just observe that you are not relaxed, automatically you begin to go in relaxation...

Feel the space around you and feel how your whole body is breathing.... just be aware of the body... just the breathing is giving you so much sensation in the body... just feel the sensation that's created in your body because of breathing... as you breathe in, something is just getting pulled inside your body and as you breathe out, something moves out... just feel the way body expands and contracts... just feel... you breathe in and the whole body expands, yes, we know the belly expands with the outgoing breath, but can you experience it? the whole body also expands... and as you breathe out, there is a feeling of contraction in the body.

Just be aware from which chakra is breathing is happening the most?... Which chakra is becoming active? Is it the Root Chakra? Is it Swadishthana? Is it Solar Plexus? Heart Chakra? Vishuddhi? 3rd eye? Crown? Which chakra is the most active right now? And that is where the breathing is going the most?.. ..

You can also feel that this particular chakra extends into the space. all our chakras are expanded in the space. It is easy to feel the active chakra in the space...

You can feel that the space is breathing too, and the way your body expands and contracts on breathing, the space is also expanding and contracting.... and that rush of energy, the rush of breathing, the rush of Prana (life force) happening not just in your body, also in the space.

Prana is rushing in the space around you, and whichever chakra is active in the space, that's what you are becoming right now.

If the Solar Plexus is expanding in the space, your whole body has become the Solar Plexus... you are Solar Plexus. That particular chakra connects with every other chakra, overrides it... Feel the rush of that vibration of that particular chakra in every other chakra and in the whole body... The whole space around you has become that chakra. And it is this chakra through which your surrounding wants to influence you... you are being impacted by your surroundings by your life through this chakra...

You can now feel the patterns that have been seeded by the world; not just now but throughout the history... just be aware of what is impacting you right now and whatever impacts you, triggers some part of your identity... some of your identities are getting triggered.

Now say thanks to the space, be in gratitude... let's open our eyes now.

Our Conditionings are Stored Inside, as well as Outside Us

Quanto Shivo: So, anyone wants to share – anything has come up???

Latha Kumar: I just felt my *Solar Plexus* expanding outside into space... and I think the sadness I was speaking about yesterday, was getting overwhelming, coming out into space... towards the end I also felt my *Heart Chakra* also expanding and I was feeling a lot of love, in spite of the sadness.

Quanto Shivo: If you can feel any *chakra*, that means, there are issues stored in there, that is why you are feeling it... when you become totally cleansed, you will not feel any *chakra*... even the *chakras* are part of your identity in the second body, the energy body... since you felt *Solar Plexus*, it means there are *Solar Plexus* issues to be resolved...

The Solar Plexus expanding into space is a very good sign... the *Solar Plexus* that has now expanded outside you into space can now interact with space... that is the way for *chakra* issues to dissolve... up till now, you were feeling the *Solar Plexus* just inside, so it can only interact with the space you can feel inside... but now the *Solar Plexus* can interact with the whole space, so that's much more intense, faster journey...

Latha Kumar: You mean that's the place where emotions are?

Quanto Shivo: You have been influenced in your past lives through *Solar Plexus* issues, the power issues... when these issues are resolved, you start to be the cosmic channel for *Solar Plexus* issues.... right now, your conditioning pathway of *Solar Plexus* is going into the space, right?... Most people say conditionings are inside us, pathways are inside us, but it is not true, from inside they are connected to outside. Because even the whole world is relating to you through your conditioning, right?... you are receiving the impact and the perception of whatever is happening in the world... isn't it?

That vibration is out in the space and it is attracting similar vibrations from everywhere. So, you can look at what kind of issues, what kind of people, you attract automatically... this is what shows your conditioning as well as the possibilities.

As *Solar Plexus* Overflows, Vibrations Move to Heart

Latha Kumar: Heart expansion is what I felt towards the end.

Quanto Shivo: Ya!!! So, as you observe... and this is the beauty, whichever *chakra* comes to your observation and begins to overflow, the *chakra* just above that will begin to get activated... since you observed the *Solar Plexus*, the vibration of that started to rise... in the observation the frequencies are already rising... reaching to the heart, the next *chakra*...

Let us understand, how the approaches of *Solar Plexus* and *Heart Chakra* are different... As the *Solar Plexus* person wants to win, wants success. The *Heart Chakra* person is happy to see people around them successful... he has already attained success, but he is also aware of the limits of that. *Solar Plexus* oriented people have a serious issue, nothing can satisfy them, nothing!!!... if you are blocked at *Solar Plexus*, if you are not reaching to the heart, nothing will satisfy you... let me mention

Alexander here, who I would say is the peak example of *Solar Plexus* conditioning.

Alexander: Crescendo of *Solar Plexus* Conditioning

Alexander wanted to win the whole world, and paradoxically, he also had an immense spiritual quest which took him to various places, masters and mystics... He was of course very atrocious, he was ferocious, the most fierce fighter, most courageous person you can ever imagine... this is what the Solar Plexus quality is... just to give an example, before Alexander, the strategy of the kings used to be to first protect themselves, and they would often wear an attire so that they are not noticed, if he is not noticed, he won't be attacked... His army was supposed to fight, not him, because if he gets killed, the fight is over, right?... So, the king would always be kept inside the protected circles of ferocious warriors...

Alexander, being the staunchest *Solar Plexus* person I can think of, reversed the whole strategy... the kind of courage he had is unimaginable... he would wear a cone shaped cap, similar to what we see on the head of circus clown in current times, that made him visible from far... this was like an invitation to attack him, everybody knew where is Alexander, his enemies knew where he was... this kind of leading from the front kept his whole army charged and motivated... his military strategies were driven by severe risk taking... So, this is the peak of Solar Plexus.

Yet, he longed for mystical moments, and that took him to various masters and mystics... Diogenes, the naked mystic of Greece, fascinated him so much, he often said, "If I was not Alexander, I would be Diogenes"... some of their conversations are recorded in history books... If you can understand Diogenes, you will become aware of the limitations of Alexander's approach to life and the *Solar Plexus* conditioning...

Diogenes is someone who is simply enjoying life, he lives naked, doesn't have any possession... the only possession he had was a bowl in which he would drink water. One day, he was walking around on the beach and he saw a boy drinking from his hand, and he realised that he can live without the bowl too, he threw his last possession away...

Let me narrate a story of Diogenes, that will help you understand his mastery... in Athens slave trade was a flourishing business, rich people would have small armies of 10-20 people, they would go around capturing people as slaves, handcuff and chain them, bring them to the market and sell them... one day, Diogenes was also captured... but, how can you capture a man, whose soul is so totally free of bondage?... This man is so free... he too was put on sale, vendors started to give call, similar to what you see in vegetable markets in India. Look at this slave, he is so healthy, he can do this work and that work and you can buy him at this much amount...

Diogenes shouted at them, "you don't even know how to sell me properly, your voice is so feeble, who is going to buy me this way, let me call for myself", and he started "Look at me – I am so healthy, can you see! And if you take me, I can do this and that and that and I am so good. I am so hardworking!"... his zeal was so much, the prospective buyers ran away, they could see, that this man is free, he can't be put in bondage... so, he couldn't be sold and his captors realised this fellow is messing up their whole business, so they pleaded with him to go.... this is obviously a man, whose Solar Plexus is awakened, but also, he knows the world beyond...

it was not surprising that his fame reached Alexander and he went to meet Diogenes... that time Diogenes was enjoying the sunbath, naked, lying on the beach... so Alexander is standing near him, waiting for Diogenes to acknowledge him, but instead Diogenes shouts, "Listen, just stay away, you are blocking the sun." And Alexander was shocked, how can anyone talk to him like that?... in another interaction, Diogenes asks him, "suppose you won the whole world, you are the king of the whole world, what will you do after that?" Suddenly there is a huge rush of realisation in Alexander... he realised, if he wins the whole world, that would be a very unfortunate day because he didn't know what he would do after that...

Latha Kumar: Nothing more to look forward to...

Quanto Shivo: This explains the *Solar Plexus* conditioning... Yes, and this is the shock for *Solar Plexus* people.... he (Alexander) was never known to be in the moment.... he was always in future, and when there is nothing to look forward to, there is a huge shock... you just keep moving from one state to another state to another state and there is no satisfaction.... this is the conditioning you will get stuck with, in *Solar Plexus*...

Whatever you achieve, or whatever you plan to achieve, nothing will satisfy you... obviously it is also a big trap because you don't stay anywhere, your plan gets bigger and bigger, and because you are always thinking of the next achievement, nothing satisfies you... grounding is so difficult in Solar Plexus...

Grounding in the Moment Happens in Heart *Chakra*, Not in *Solar Plexus*

In heart, the grounding is easy, because you start to enjoy whatever is there around you, the world around you... the *Heart Chakra* person would even enjoy the *Solar Plexus* people and feel compassionate towards them, he knows the struggle, the fights, the travails, the issues that a *Solar Plexus* person goes through... and that's why they are the one who create many heroes, *Lord Krishna* is the perfect example of this... *Krishna* creates so many heroes, because he has lived the *Solar Plexus* and he is now grounded in *Heart Chakra*... *Rajsuya Yagnu*, that was conducted by *Yudhishthir* is the perfect example, if *Krishna* wanted, he could have done it for himself and become the emperor, the superior to all of kings of contemporary *Bharatha*, yet he asks *Yudhishthir* to conduct that yagna...

Latha Kumar: So, observing the *Solar Plexus* and becoming aware helps your *Heart Chakra* to become grounded?

Quanto Shivo: Not grounded, but if you observe the *Solar Plexus*, the *Heart Chakra* will begin to awaken, and eventually it will get grounded at some point... once you begin to get free from *Solar Plexus* issues, you begin to move into the *Heart Chakra*... Are you able to relate?

Latha Kumar: Yes!!! Yes!!! very much!!!

Quanto Shivo: What are the issues that come up for you?

Latha Kumar: For me the issue is, I have always worked towards setting goals and moving forward. All my life I have worked from *Solar Plexus*… there is no end to it.

Quanto Shivo: And nothing would satisfy you …right?

Latha Kumar: No, nothing would satisfy… And now due to my spiritual seeking, I am actually acknowledging the *Heart Chakra*… A feeling of love and seeing everybody else successful is also moving forward. It is a very deep part of my awareness now.

Quanto Shivo: So, one of the major conditionings of *Solar Plexus* you need to observe is, do you enjoy life?… it's very difficult for a *Solar Plexus* person to enjoy life, you only live to achieve, not to enjoy… but what happens in the end… So, Alexander was dying at age of 28, he had won a big part of the world and then there was a strange disease that overtook him and put him on deathbed… he decided that it was time to go back to his home… He loved his mother a lot, he knew he is going to die, so he wanted to see his mother desperately… he was about to reach Athens, he pleaded to his doctors for just one more day, and he was ready to give up his whole kingdom in return… And the doctors expressed their limitations that they could not do that… And then he said that let the world know that Alexander who was the greatest king ever, also went empty handed… so, he said in his last wish: "when my body is being taken around, keep both my hands outside, palms open so that people come to know even I am going empty-handed… every *Solar Plexus* person need to imbibe this knowing that when we go, we go empty handed, and if you have not enjoyed life then it would appear a total waste.

Latha Kumar: Actually, now I am in a different phase, but that has been a very strong part of my conditioning, thank you sir!!!

Quanto Shivo: Thank you Latha for sharing this, can I also ask the others if they have experienced the *Solar Plexus* conditionings?

Unreal Strategies Are a Trap

Ruchi: I also experienced *Solar Plexus* and *Heart Chakra* expanding... I felt as if it was raining outside. There was this beautiful smell coming from outside. Though in the beginning, I could smell a pungent smell, just for a second, and it was gone.

Quanto Shivo: The sweet smell is of *Heart Chakra* and pungent is of *Solar Plexus*... that also tells me Ruchi that your sense of smell is very active and this could be a valuable part of your *sadhana* (meditative practice) ... You can feel the space through smell, close your eyes and maybe smell the space, like we feel the space... Yeah! go ahead!!!

Ruchi: Yeah!!! And in the light of the story of Alexander, I can see that I am never satisfied... I don't enjoy my victory at all, if I reach here (shows the palm as a benchmark), what's the big deal, I should have been there (moves the palm a little higher) ... that makes me feel like a failure... this year I doubled my business, but still the feeling is, what is the big deal, in so many years where have I reached???... I am not able to really enjoy!

Quanto Shivo: Also, the trap is, it gives you strategy and planning that can become unreal at any point... Alexander too went into this trap, that is why he had to return back... there is another story I want to share, which will probably help everyone to understand this trap...

Once a king was pleased with someone, and he offered him a generous reward, whatever land he can circle before sunset, becomes his... Now tell me, what would happen to this person?

Ruchi: He would die... he would just be running, running all the time, panting and then ultimately just collapse.

Quanto Shivo: Yes true, but another question is, would he complete any circle???... Can someone tell me, would this man complete the circle?... If you want to understand the traps of *Solar Plexus*, understand this story, it tells you what your future is.

Rajkumari Sahariya: He doesn't complete the circle sir... he keeps running, running, hoping that he will gain more land, and he believes that he will be able to complete the circle and get more land... but he can't reach back and then collapses...

Quanto Shivo: He will also not be able to come back before sunset... in his greed, he wants to run to far off, he is unrealistic, and he runs so far, reaching a point, from where he can't complete the circle before sunset... he has bitten more than he can chew, hence he ends up getting no land... his greed has forced him into unrealistic dreams, into unrealistic planning, and he is trapped... this is the state of every *Solar Plexus* person.

Ruchi: Yeah, so this is how I can relate, there is no satisfaction... just chasing, chasing, chasing the mirage, the *maya*.

Quanto Shivo: This is how you are describing now, when you reflect back, when you are feeling desperate... but go back into that time, when you were planning... did you say this that time, I am chasing *maya*, I am chasing mirage?

Ruchi: It's so real, and I know it now... I can also experience moments, where I am not enjoying that... I think very *Solar Plexus* like, as I can understand now.

Contempt: Symptom of Solar Unconsciousness

Rajkumari Sahariya: Sir, I could not feel the *Solar Plexus*... the only *chakra* which I felt was the *Crown Chakra*, and it was actually absorbing all the *chakras* within me, it was just expanding and expanding... then when you said go to the *Solar Plexus*, I actually had to search for it in my *Crown Chakra*... as I was searching, my energy went to the *Heart Chakra* and from there again jumped back to the *Crown Chakra*... and I was totally there thinking, why do I need to go to any other *chakra,* as I felt full and complete, completely at peace with myself... tell me something why was this happening?

Quanto Shivo: There are two possibilities, either you have crossed *Solar Plexus* or it has not awakened yet... and the way to test is, if you feel comfortable with the successful people, even if you are much less successful than them... if you are totally ok with people much more successful than you, then you have crossed it...

I have seen a lot of people say, that they are *Santoshi Jeev* (content beings), they quote the sayings like *"Santoshi hi paramdhan hai"* (contentment is the ultimate wealth), *"Santoshi sada sukhi"* (content being is always happy)... you also must have met such people... this was the common moral that used to be prevalent in middle class salaried people, many of you must have had parents in jobs, especially in government jobs, they often said, we are content people, are don't get into dirty games of money... so how do we know, if they are really content with their lives, or is it just an excuse because going after money is very risky?...

I have seen many such people, full of condemnation for ambitious people, they would say, "Oh! see, how much money that person has made in dirty ways!" ... and when you watch their faces, they seem very angry... definitely such people are not content. It is just an excuse, they are scared of taking risks in life... for such people, even though their needs are satisfied, the greed is still there... contempt is the symptom that your Solar Plexus is yet unconscious...

Rajkumari Sahariya: Yeah!!!, so I can tell you, just yesterday I went to an award ceremony... there were many women of substance there... even though I was not involved in the ceremony, my name was called out to give the award to someone, and actually I was feeling so happy, seeing those ladies reach those places... there was nothing like where am I, nothing... I was actually in euphoria, wow, they have done it, they have reached the zenith... there was nothing like jealousy or anything of that sort, because I felt I always did the best of my abilities. I reached where I reached, there was no comparison or something.

Quanto Shivo: Wonderful!!!...Yeah! comparison or the sense of competition, is one of the biggest issues, we face at *Solar Plexus*... that is a block. Let's say, someone arrives in your organisation more capable than you... check whether you feel happy about it or you feel threatened.... A person who is at *vishuddhi chakra* will be happy because for him the joy is in learning, he is happy because he has an opportunity to learn from such a knowledgeable person... but the person who is still at the *Solar Plexus*, not connected to the heart is thinking, "What happens to my promotion now?... this is a simple way to check the state of your *Solar Plexus*.

Vibrations Attract and Reinforce Themselves

Anonymous 2: I have grown up with super intelligent parents, but they were always victimised... my mother always said that mediocre people always get better pay, so financially they are always better off, people who are intelligent and hard working are always victims... there was a woman, who wanted to pull her down, and that I feel has become such a strong part of me... my thing is, if you are good, if you are intelligent, if you are talented, you are pulled down.

Quanto Shivo: And of course, that is what is happening with you again and again, and your belief system is getting reinforced with every instance... do you see, this vibrational field of this belief is becoming stronger day by day... you experienced the *Solar Plexus* extended into the space, and these vibrations are attracting these circumstances... you are attracting these circumstances like a magnet... this belief is your personal truth, which attracts evidences to prove itself correct...

Anonymous 2: Do I attract those circumstances? Rather I think, I get attracted to them.

Quanto Shivo: Yes, you attract those and you get attracted to those... both are the same.

Good Girl Syndrome: Strategy to Gain Approval

Anonymous 2: As you asked, what is your core identity? I am not sure, whether my identity is of a victim, or it is to be the good girl? I was always a good girl; kind of sacrificial lamb... my mother used to say, "let your cousin have it, she is not that well-mannered, you are well-mannered, no"? You are my good girl, so you give in... it could be my dress or a seat in the car or whatever it was… so my thing became, If I sacrifice, I get appreciation… So now what is my core identity?

Quanto Shivo: Yeah, so these are the two sides of your identity. Right?… There is the act of sacrifice, and you are also rewarded in terms of approval.

Anonymous 2: Yes! Yes!… and I love that approval.

Quanto Shivo: Yeah… because you love that approval, your sacrifice is going to continue. There is no other way… you yourself have chosen that strategy, even though it was an unconscious choice.

Anonymous 2: Like I had shared earlier, I sacrificed a lot for my husband, I am ready to do for him whatever he says… because I had seen my mother take my father's place when we were in Pune, she was the head of the house, she gave us love, she gave us everything, she held the fort together… I also did what my mother did, we were going through extremely trying times, in terms of finance from the time I got married, every time I became more than his wife, I became the mother.

Quanto Shivo: Yeah, you had a strong desire to be like your mother… she was your role model…

Anonymous 2: Yes! she is my role model.

Quanto Shivo: So what works for you is, "I will sacrifice and I will gain approval in return…" This is the life you chose unconsciously, and this is the life that is manifesting for you… when you chose it, you were not aware that there will be a heavy cost you have to pay to gain approval… since gaining approval was crucial for your survival, you kept paying the cost, you kept sacrificing, now you are calling yourself a victim… this is already an open secret for everyone around you, that you will sacrifice to gain approval, so it's easy for them to take advantage of you…. You are a victim, not so much of the people or life, but of your own conditioning… If you want to let go of this being victim, you also have to let go of your hunger for approval… you have to let go of both of them at the same time.

Anonymous 2: Meaning victim and approval?

Quanto Shivo: Yes! Victimhood and approval, both has to go at the same time.... you want to keep the approval, but let go of victimhood, and that is not possible... You can't let go of approval, because that is your way to survive, that is why, you can't let go of your victimhood... this hunger for approval is your core identity....

Anonymous 2: Yes Shivo...Because, you know what, I did so much for almost over 20 years...

Quanto Shivo: Now you are going into the stories... can you see how your identity is forcing you to move away from crux?... Just be present to this, right? Recall the events that are coming up for you, okay?

The *Lakshmi* Woman Turns Her Man into a Grand Success

Vaibhav: Sir, don't *Heart Chakra* people have ambitions?

Quanto Shivo: They are ambitious; but they are the masters. Ambition don't own them, rather they own ambitions.... the problem with the Solar Plexus people is, they don't have ambition, rather ambition has them, understand?... They are not the master, when the ambition comes, they have no choice, they cannot say no to it... Heart Chakra person, on the other hand, can say no to it... That's why the Heart Chakra person will always be more real... And that is why every Solar Plexus should have a Heart Chakra person in their life, if they want to avoid disasters.

I have spoken about the *Lakshmi* women before too... Lakshmi women is the one who brings great luck for her man.... this is not just by chance, but she has that kind of a character, that her man is bound to become successful... she is the one who is so much centred at heart, and that's why her men become successful... on the contrary, if it is a Swadishthana woman, the pleasure oriented one, she will pull down a successful man into disaster... a Heart Chakra woman will pull up a man who is in a disaster into success... So, if you are a Solar Plexus person and you find it hard to move up to Heart Chakra, at least have some Heart Chakra people in your life. Right? Vaibhav, does that answer your question?

Vaibhav: Yes Sir! Somewhat.

Fear of Chaos: The *Vishshudhi Chakra* Block

Jeet: I resonated so much with the sharing on loneliness yesterday... this has been happening with me too, for the past many years... I have shared it in the past and so many in Quanto Life know this... I have had this feeling, that I don't belong here, I have come from some other planet, I have always felt that deep loneliness and disassociation... however, what I didn't realise before, that it was not loneliness and longing, not the disassociation from the world... so I recognised that today, I got this deep insight and message, "Jeet, when you can't accept the world, the planet Earth, it's people, when you have resistance towards that, how are you expecting them to accept you?"... I just wanted to share with everybody, because this is something that opened up here yesterday...

I also had a realisation in today's session, which is sort of very collective, few others will also feel it along with me... and that is the fear of tomorrow... yes there is so much advancement in everything in life, be it AI (Artificial Intelligence), the finance... we could not do these kinds of sessions before... all this is great, but there is a lot of fear too, the fear of tomorrow, where am I going to be tomorrow... "where am I? where do I exist in this?"... this, I suppose is a very Root Chakra thing.

Quanto Shivo: Fear of chaos is basically the block of *Vishudhi Chakra*, this is the fear of unknown.

Jeet: And a fear of self, like "I don't know how good am I, Can I make it? Will I be good enough to make it"? Right?

Quanto Shivo: Here along with the fear of unknown, the *Vishshudhi Chakra* block, the *Solar Plexus* block has got mixed up too, which is doubting your own power, may be the *Root Chakra* block too: "Will I able to survive here?" Is it so Jeet? Observe all the blocks together as one reality.

Be One with Life: Drop the Will and Determination

Jyotsana: *Pranam Shivo...* how do we know which *chakra* person we are?

Quanto Shivo: Close your eyes, just breathe deep... See where the Consciousness is moving to, or just see which *chakra* begins to breathe... just observe. Okay? so you can observe and come back...

Kawal: *Pranam* Shivo! I felt my *Root Chakra* expanding, and it went little bit into *sacral*... normally when everybody is talking, I do feel so numb, I feel my heart is closed, I have been feeling this for many years now.

Quanto Shivo: So Kawal, at this stage, you are facing a lot of survival issues... the coexistence has become difficult.

Kawal: Yeah, a lot has been going on in my life for a couple of years.

Quanto Shivo: Become present to your *Root Chakra*, the *Root Chakra* expanded into space... feel your *Root Chakra* survival issues in the whole Space... and those will begin to dissolve quickly... be present to that... Yes, Jyotsana, you want to say something? Did you feel which *chakra* is breathing?

Jyotsana: Crown Chakra.

Quanto Shivo: All right, so that's what needs your attention right now... just feel that.

Jyotsana: Okay, so how should I relate it with the present situation?

Quanto Shivo: It could be the longing to become one with life... the issue here is that you feel disconnected with life... here, I am feeling your father so much, you saw your father trusting life so much, right? and you have been kind of wanting to be in the same space like him, he is your inspiration... but that has not happened yet, that trust in life has not happened for you... and it's because, probably you intellectualised a lot of things... I remember, long time back you ascribed what your father was, to his will and determination... and that is how you tried to live your life.... but it was just your interpretation, and not the truth... the truth is, it was not the will and determination, but the complete trust in life, surrender to life... Am I making sense here?... and that is not working for you... So, you need to let go of that will and determination... You have lived life believing that if you have will and determination, everything will work in life.

Jyotsana: Yes, but is that not true?

Quanto Shivo: That is not working for you... for some people it may work, okay? For you it is not working... that is what the Crown Chakra block is suggesting.

Jyotsana: Then what should I do?

Quanto Shivo: If you are longing to become one with life, then this will and determination is not going to work for you... So can you just close your eyes, feel this huge surge of energy in your third eye... can you just feel it? It is longing to move up.

So for everyone; wherever your energy is, the most intense energy is, it is longing to move to the next higher *chakra*.. however, don't try to make it move... efforts are not going to work... but just be present... and this consciousness you bring in by being present, that itself is enough for energy to get moving, wherever it is supposed to move.... just in observation, energy will begin to rise... The next chakra will open up.... may be, it will open up today itself, or maybe later... crux is to be in observation... ok, Jyotsana? thank you!!!

Kawal: Shivo, I forgot to ask you something... I feel a lot of incompleteness and loneliness.

Quanto Shivo: The loneliness is because of the block in *Swadhisthana*, like we discussed with Shweta yesterday... you feel loneliness because energy is blocked in *Root Chakra*... as the energy begins to rise to *sacral chakra*, the loneliness issue will begin to resolve... so be present to the *Root Chakra*... and be present where it is blocked ...right? Thank you!

Drop Wishing, Waiting, Hopes, Prayers; Get into Action

Quanto Shivo: Yes Rashi! your turn.

Rashi: Ummm... You are going to ask me, how am I feeling in this moment?

Quanto Shivo: Yeah, what is the truth of this moment for you?

Rashi: uh!!!... I don't know!!!

Quanto Shivo: Is that the truth of the moment for you - I don't know? Is that how you feel about life, I don't know?... what is the emotion you feel, with this I don't know?

Rashi: Freedom!!

Quanto Shivo: Does it really give you freedom, or does it give you fear?

Rashi: No, it doesn't give me fear... it gives me freedom.

Quanto Shivo: Then what is the issue?... I mean, you are feeling free, it means you are already in space, nothing is restricting you, you are practically grounded.

Rashi: (chuckling)... I don't think! I am that much great...

Quanto Shivo: No, it's not about being great... Alexander was great, but he was not free...

Rashi: What to say!!!

Quanto Shivo: So, Rashi, you are confused... I feel you are very confused.

Rashi: Maybe!

Quanto Shivo: So that's the truth of this moment for you... there are changes that are happening, and you just don't know how to deal with that... You are just confused... There are choices to be made, actions to be taken... But there is so much conflict in your own heart, in your own mind... so much conflict is going around, that you are in the state of inaction and you are in the state of I don't know, this is not same as rejoicing in I don't know, celebrating I don't know... It's a state of confusion.

Rashi: It's a state of waiting...confusion and waiting, yeah!!!

Quanto Shivo: Yeah!!! So, it's like something will happen that life will automatically get sorted, right?... there is waiting, there is also expectations that life will go certain way, the positive way...

Rashi: it's not expecting... it's umm! wishing... and a prayer!

Quanto Shivo: Wishing!!!... Yeah!!!... And that is why it is not happening, you are wishing, you are not in action, and you are waiting. If you drop wishing, the reality will become apparent to you... so you need to drop wishing... so, what are you hoping for?

Rashi: Shivo, at this stage, it's all around my son Karthik... nothing else is coming to mind...

Quanto Shivo: Yeah!!!, and you have certain hopes that things will resolve by itself.

Rashi: Yeah! because there is a lot of confusion, there is no guidance around.

Quanto Shivo: This is a pattern, and it is coming from your past... When you are faced with difficult situations, you hope... Is that how you have lived?... whenever there is a difficult situation in front of you, you hope... see, hope doesn't allow you to be present to the situation... If you want to be present to the situation, you need to feel the crisis of that... on the contrary, what you are doing is, you are using hope to avoid the crisis, you don't want to feel the crisis, you don't want to acknowledge that there is a crisis... and the way you are doing this is by hoping.

Rashi: Yeah! I am doing it by hoping, plus I am doing some actions, but results will come at their own time, so there is a period of a lot of anxiety, what will happen, how it will happen, all that is going on, and everything is all around that.

Quanto Shivo: Rashi can you be present to the way you are hoping?... Can you also be present to the consequences of your various choices, for example if I take this action, these could be the positive and negative consequences and if I don't act at all what could be the positive and negative consequences... the gap I am feeling is, that, you have become present to what good can come out of this action, but you are not present to what negative can happen out of it... you could either choose action or inaction, both will have negative and positive consequences... are you getting it? This is the gap, what negative could happen is not present in your consciousness, and that is why you are falling again and again, that is why you are getting trapped again and again, because you never thought that things could go in that negative fashion... this pattern is really attacking you...

Rashi: I can't understand anything, Shivo...

Quanto Shivo: Mansi, would you like to say something here???... (Amused tone) Rashi's face looks like, the thunderstorm is passing all around her, but she is not even taking notice... Rashi, you are feeling numb... You are feeling very insensitive to what is happening around you. Mansi, do you want to say something?

Quanto Mansi: Yes Shivo!! She is like that Rasogulla in sugar syrup, but it is not able to absorb it, because its outer surface has no pores for it to enter... (laughing) I mean guys look at her, doesn't she feel like that Rasogulla?

Being Numb is a Bad Strategy to Face Life

Quanto Shivo: We had this interaction with Vaibhav yesterday... something similar... do you remember it Rashi?... there is so much uncertainty in life, you can adopt an unconscious strategy, to become numb, not to feel anything... and this is how you have also responded in past also, when you face a very difficult situation, you become numb... I cannot feel anything. and if you cannot feel anything, then there is no crisis, right?... things are going bad, everything is collapsing, but you cannot feel anything, so there is no problem, right?... such a good strategy, or is that really good?... Rashi, I am immensely enjoying looking at you... like a house elder, you tell her that this problem is coming, she will only smile...

Vaibhav: Sir is that not trust in life?

Quanto Shivo: This is not trust... trust is, I am open... I am ready to feel everything that life brings to me, including the negative, I am ready to go through all the crisis. You understand?... and I know that if I go through that crisis, it is going to be good for me... on the contrary, being numb is, I don't want to feel the crisis, so I just make up in my mind that everything is perfect, because I don't feel it.

Vaibhav: But sir, isn't this such a good way?

Quanto Shivo: Really??...huh???

Vaibhav: Yes! it is a good way... I mean, for the sake of some peace, this is a good way...

Sakha: Only you can say this Vaibhav (giggles)

Quanto Shivo: (Laughing)... I have never seen you like this Rashi.. honestly!

Rashi: Shivo, what happened to you???

Quanto Shivo: Really! I mean, you are feeling like a plastic doll, sitting in front of me, like a robot, and she is laughing too... put her on charging, and she will get charged too... honestly, you are looking like someone programmed, and not feeling anything.... and this is because you have adopted the strategy to avoid everything that could be bad... even if something bad happens, it doesn't affect me...I am numb...

Rashi: Yes, actually Shivo you are right, I am kind of, I was thinking about it yesterday, if something worse happens to me, how will I react? I was like, it's ok...

Quanto Shivo: So, Rashi can you feel this numbness, and fear of what you may begin to feel, if you are not numb...

Synthesis Process for Dissolving *Chakra* Blocks

So I invite everyone to feel where you are right now,... what is the truth of this moment for you???

Which *chakra* became active for you?... can you recall the events related with that *chakra* or the emotion which is bursting out?

If your energies are moving up from somewhere, from some *chakra* and not reaching the next *chakra*, just be present... Just be in the observation of your block, energies will find its way... In your observation, all blocks dissolve... Feel the whole energy structure... chakras... whichever are active or inactive...just be in observation...

I am also feeling the numbness in the whole of the Quanto field right now.. just be present and be present to the fact that numbness is the result of fear for future, or fear for the present, unwillingness to accept what is going on... feel that numbness...

Let's invoke the Quanto field: Quanto!!!. .. Quanto!!!...Quanto!!!

In this whole space of observation and awareness, you can begin to feel that something from outside, from space, is pushing into you.

Let's go into deep *Shavasan* and let's go into the sleep.

Thank you very much for joining today!!!

GLOSSARY OF TERMS

1. ***Ashwathama***: is an illustrious warrior from epic *Mahabharat* who ends up carrying the worst curse ever.

2. ***Aura***: it is the energy field representing the second of the seven bodies mostly spread a little outside of the physical body.

3. ***Bhagvad Gita***: the most referred to and revered Hindu text in modern times. It has the most number of commentaries and interpretations written by a vast diaspora.

4. ***Death card***: is the thirteenth major card in the traditional tarot system symbolising transformation, sudden unexpected change, the potential for deep let go of old patterns and ways that no longer serve us.

5. ***Dwapar yuga***: The period of second lowest consciousness where forces of good and evil are almost in balance.

6. ***Imprints:*** impressions of how concentrated vibrations of individual and collective subconscious are stored inside and outside the body.

7. ***Kali Yuga***: the period of lowest consciousness in the *yuga* cycle where evil rules and world disintegrates.

8. ***Karma/karmic:*** it is the principle of cause and effect. Every action has its own inevitable ramifications.

9. ***Mahavakyas (maha - great, vakyas - sentences)***: are the most vital sutras containing the deepest wisdom in the *Upanishads*.

10. ***Quanto Asaan***: facilitates you to be open and vulnerable for interaction with space. It is similar to *Ardha Padmasana* where both the feet are exposed.

11. ***Quanto Mudra:*** is keeping your palms on your knees- open to the skies.

12. ***Rasgulla:*** an indian dessert, sweet dumpling.

13. ***Sutra:*** It is a formula that opens the door to a new understanding.

14. ***Shavasana:*** the corpse pose - of letting go and complete relaxation. Most yoga and meditation practices end with *shavasana*.

15. ***Tat Tvam Asi:*** You are also that - is one of the four great sentences of the *Upanishads*. It is the followup to *Aham Brahmaasmi* - I am God.

16. ***The Tower card***: is the sixteenth major card in the traditional tarot system. The Tower moment is the time and space when the tower of false assumptions is struck down by reality. The tower may have seemed mighty but now it falls down as a pack of cards.

17. ***Upanishads:*** Along with *Vedas*, the *Upanishads* are the oldest and most revered Hindu scriptures. *Upanishads* contain the peak wisdom on consciousness, ontology and mechanism of life.

18. ***Yagna:*** is to revere divinity with fire rituals.

19. ***Yuga***: A cycle of consciousness of duration of 24,000 years, mentioned in Hindu scriptures.

20. ***Chakras:*** English / Sanskrit names of energy centres:

Sahasrar	–	Crown
Ajna	–	Third eye
Vishuddhi	–	Throat
Anahat	–	Heart
Manipur	–	Solar Plexus
Swadishthan	–	Sacral
Mooladhar	–	Root

ABOUT QUANTO SHIVO

Quanto Shivo is an evolution alchemist, he metamorphosized into a cosmic channel through his extremely intense spiritual journey and deep surrender to God.

Shivo has channeled a plethora of ground breaking concepts in diverse fields such as Ascending Dwapar consciousness * Plasmic Era * Grounding In Space * Quanto Synthesis Process * Evolutionary dimensions of various gods / goddesses and their invocation processes * empowerment of deva souls * Conscious pilgrimage * 84 mahadev-84 dimensions of consciousness * Entity liberation * Reincarnation Ontology * Ego consciousness cycles on life after life journey * Accelerated Karma cleansing * Dissolving Collective Subconscious * Identity Dynamics and Paradoxes * Collective vibrational fields * Deva healing * Quantum Entrepreneurship * Soul families * Nurturing of unique individual fragrance * Synthesis of paradoxes * Wisdom circles * Heart space / mind space as the key asset in knowledge era * Spotting human potential that AI (Artificial Intelligence) can't reach.

He is also the creator of Quantum Astrology, Astro Power Yantra, spacetime astrological model for earth event predictions, 50 year consciousness cycle.

He is the founder of Quanto Life- the spiritual path for chaotic times. He is the revered and beloved guide for many more cosmic channels, in the process and heroes whose potential he has unearthed and nurtured.

He is an engg graduate from prestigious MNIT, Jaipur, and has been through diverse careers- economic journalism, equity research, web strategist and visionary, career astrology coach at TV9 show.

*****